ILLUSTRATED GUIDE TO THE
WILDFLOWERS
OF NORTHERN SOUTH AFRICA

Supported by the
National Botanical Institute

ILLUSTRATED GUIDE TO THE
WILDFLOWERS
OF NORTHERN SOUTH AFRICA

Text by Gerrit Germishuizen

Paintings by Brenda Clarke

BRIZA

Published by

BRIZA PUBLICATIONS
CK 90/11690/23
PO Box 56569
Arcadia 0007
Pretoria
South Africa

First edition, first impression, 2003

Copyright © in text: Gerrit Germishuizen
Copyright © in paintings: Brenda Clarke
Copyright © in published edition: Briza Publications

All rights reserved. No part of this publication may be reproduced or transmitted in any form or by any means without written permission of the copyright holders.

ISBN 1 875093 39 7

Disclaimer

Although care has been taken to be as accurate as possible, neither the author nor the publisher makes any expressed or implied representation as to the accuracy of the information contained in this book and cannot be held legally responsible or accept liability for any errors or omissions.

Managing editor: Reneé Ferreira
Copy-editor: Emsie du Plessis
Cover design: Sally Whines, The Departure Lounge
Typesetting: Melinda Stark, Lebone Publishing Services
Reproduction: Doc Colour, Randburg
Printed and bound by Tien Wah Press (Pte.) Ltd, Singapore

This book is in memory of Percy Clarke

Contents

Author's acknowledgements   8

Introduction   9
    Nomenclature   10
    Abbreviations   11
    Distribution throughout northern South Africa   12
    Habitat symbols   12

Family descriptions   13

Notes   24

Illustrated guide   25

    White/Cream-coloured flowers   26

    Pink flowers   68

    Yellow/Orange flowers   90

    Blue flowers   144

    Mauve/Purple flowers   154

    Red flowers   186

    Brown flowers   196

    Green flowers   200

Glossary   206

Literature references and further reading   212

Index to scientific names   214

Index to common names   222

Author's acknowledgements

A book of this nature cannot be compiled without the assistance of many people.

I offer a special thanks to the artist and dear friend Brenda Clarke for all her beautiful, accurate illustrations of flowering plants of the region as well as for the collecting and drying of most of the voucher specimens. I am also grateful to her late husband, Percy, who supported and assisted her in this project, which involved much travelling to various localities throughout northern South Africa to obtain different flowering species.

A special word of thanks to Jessica Clarke for her generous assistance and to Patricia Barnard for the introduction to Briza Publications, both making this publication possible.

My thanks also go to Miss Eleanor-Mary Cadell for her initial ideas on a book of this nature as well as her encouragement in its compilation.

I am extremely grateful to the former Director, Dr B. de Winter, and to former and current staff of the National Botanical Institute (formerly the Botanical Research Institute), particularly Dr D.J.B. Killick, Mrs B.J. Pienaar, Miss E. Retief, Miss W.H. Welman, Mrs M.C. Crosby, Mrs E. du Plessis, Mr P.P.J. Herman, Mrs C.M. van Wyk, Mr A. Balsinhas, Mrs M. Jordaan, Mrs C. Archer, Dr B.D. Schrire, Dr K.L. Immelman, Dr H.F. Glen, Mrs M. Dednam, and the late Mr D. Hardy who supplied a collection of live succulent plants for illustration. I thank Dr K. Balkwill of the Moss Herbarium, Johannesburg, for his assistance in identifying material of the Acanthaceae family and giving useful hints on how to separate the different taxa from one another. Gill Condy, resident artist of the Institute, is thanked for illustrating the habitat symbols and for checking the colour proofs.

Last but not least, my thanks go to my parents, family and friends for all their encouragement and help.

GERRIT GERMISHUIZEN

Introduction

The idea for the *Illustrated guide to the wildflowers of northern South Africa* started several years ago when the author and artist realised that, although there were a number of books on the subject of the wild flowers of northern South Africa, there was still a great need for an illustrated pocket guide that could be easily carried into the field by botanists, nature lovers, ecotourists, hikers and farmers, for on-the-spot identifications, making it unnecessary to collect specimens and deplete the countryside of its beautiful natural heritage.

Although this publication overlaps to some extent with *Wild flowers of the Transvaal* by Cythna Letty, *Transvaal wild flowers* and *Wild flowers of northern South Africa* by Anita Fabian & Gerrit Germishuizen, it offers a greater variety of flowering plants, succulents and shrublets, rarely shrubs. It contains a total of 90 families, 330 genera and 614 taxa illustrated in full colour. The arrangement follows the order set out in the two volumes of *The genera of southern African flowering plants* by R.A. Dyer published in 1975 and 1976 and in *Seed plants of southern Africa: families and genera* by O.A. Leistner (editor) in *Strelitzia* 10 published in 2000.

The species, subspecies and variety names are according to *Plants of southern Africa: names and distribution* by T.H. Arnold & B.C. de Wet (editors) published in 1993. They are placed in eight major colour categories, namely white/cream-coloured flowers, pink flowers, yellow/orange flowers, blue flowers, mauve/purple flowers, red flowers, brown flowers and green flowers. These categories are based on the general colour impression of the flower. In many species the flowers have more than one colour form and these are then mentioned under each taxon. Within each of the colour categories the species fall under their respective families.

The more well known exotic or alien weeds, such as Californian poppy, cosmos, garden ageratum, Mexican poppy, pom-pom weed, redstar zinnia and wild verbena, have also been included in this publication to make the reader aware of the spread of these competitive plants in our natural vegetation.

As a result of the large number of taxa that are included, the text is presented as concisely as possible, with symbols indicating the habitat of each species. English and Afrikaans vernacular names are included where appropriate. The plant families relevant to this book are briefly introduced, in alphabetical order, where possible giving characters to distinguish them from each other. To make botanical terms more comprehensible to the lay person, a botanical glossary is provided on page 206. Separate indexes for scientific and common names are given at the end of the book.

Northern South Africa for the purposes of this publication covers the four northern provinces: Limpopo, North-West, Gauteng and Mpumalanga, occupying roughly an area of 325 000 km^2 north of the Vaal River and supporting a diversity of flora. The region extends from about 22° 40' to 32° 00' E and from 22° 10' to 28° 00' S. The altitude ranges from about 300 m in the lowveld in the east, to the wide plains of the Kalahari basin around 1 000 m in the west, the extensive highveld between 1 500 and 2 000 m, to the highest mountain peaks of the eastern escarpment at about 2 300 m.

The climate, which is temperate in winter with frost on the highveld and hot in summer when the region receives most of its annual rainfall, plays an important role in the distribution of certain species. There are two distinct rainfall zones, namely the western zone with 380 to 710 mm average rainfall and the eastern zone with 500 to 1 000 mm per annum. The western zone stretches from the Limpopo River valley to the Waterberg Mountains, while the eastern zone encompasses the escarpment and the lowveld. Both areas support an abundance of plant types specially adapted to local conditions.

According to Rutherford & Westfall (1994), there are two major biomes found in northern South Africa, the Grassland Biome and the Savanna Biome. The grassland, roughly making up 16.52 % of South Africa's vegetation, is largely restricted to the highveld in the central and southern parts of this region as far as the eastern escarpment. The areas to the north, west and east are mostly classified as savanna (locally known as bushveld), representing roughly 46.16 % of South Africa's vegetation cover. These biomes can be broken up into smaller units known as veld types. Grassland can be subdivided into sweet, mixed and sour grassveld according to Acocks (1988) and he furthermore recognises a few areas of forest/scrubforest on the eastern escarpment. Sweet grassland (grassveld) is usually restricted to the region receiving less than 600 mm rain per annum, whereas sour grassland is found in the moister regions, with mixed grassland in the intermediate regions. Fire is a frequent occurrence in both savanna and grassland and most plants can withstand the effect of fire.

It is interesting to note that most of South Africa's nature and game reserves are found in northern South Africa. Added to this are the mountains and scenic splendour of the lowveld of Mpumalanga and Limpopo Provinces that attract tourists to the region from all over the world.

Nomenclature

The text contains the scientific names of both the genus and the species, as laid down by the International Code of Botanical Nomenclature, which eliminates any confusion that might arise. In general, the oldest specific name is the valid one and therefore changes often have to be made as research discloses an earlier description. Inevitably, too, generic name changes occur as taxonomic revisions are undertaken. More well known synonyms of the species names are provided in brackets.

Abbreviations

aff.:	affinity
cf.:	closest to, nearest to certain species
Distr:	distribution
Fl:	flowering season
Ht:	height of plant
ined.:	unpublished
sp.:	species
subsp.:	subspecies
T:	throughout northern South Africa
var.:	variety
±:	approximately, more or less

Distribution throughout northern South Africa

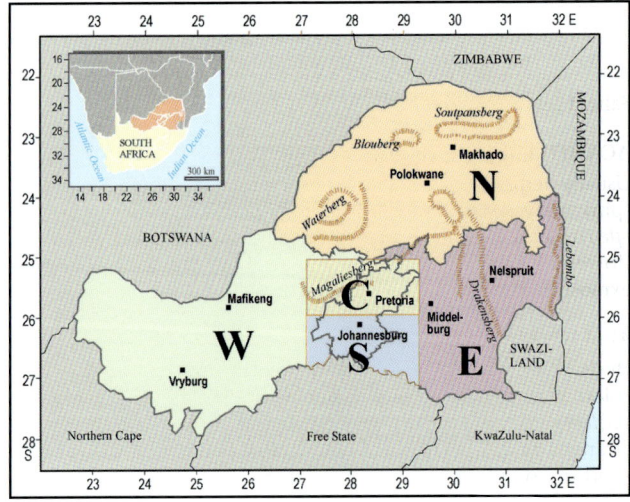

C: central parts (mostly Gauteng Province)
E: eastern parts (mostly Mpumalanga Province)
N: northern parts (mostly Limpopo Province)
S: southern parts (mostly Gauteng Province)
W: western parts (mostly North-West Province)

Habitat symbols

- Grassland
- Bushveld
- Forest
- Rocky places
- Slopes
- By water
- Roadsides
- (R) Rare
- (W) Weed
- (E) Exotic

Family descriptions

Salient features are in italics.

ACANTHACEAE Acanthus Family
Usually herbs, shrublets, shrubs or sometimes climbers; sometimes spiny. Leaves simple, opposite. *Bracts and bracteoles conspicuous, often coloured and sometimes spiny*, usually subtending the individual flowers. Flowers bisexual, irregular, 1- or 2-lipped. Fruit an explosive, club-shaped or ellipsoid capsule.

ALLIACEAE Onion Family
Herbaceous, spreading perennials, often forming clumps or colonies from bulbs or bulb-like corms; usually *emitting a strong smell of garlic when crushed*. Leaves concentrated at the base, spirally arranged or rarely in two ranks. Inflorescence umbel-like with short- or long-stalked flowers. Perianth segments 3 + 3.

AMARANTHACEAE Amaranth Family
Annual or perennial herbs or shrublets. Leaves alternate or opposite, simple, entire, without stipules. Flowers bisexual or unisexual, may be solitary or in spike- or head-like inflorescences, usually surrounded by *dry, chaffy, often spinescent bracts*, often showy in masses. Tepals 1–3 or 5, free, dry, membranous to firm. *Petals absent*.

AMARYLLIDACEAE Amaryllis Family
Perennial or biennial herbs, mostly bulbous with thick fleshy scales, occasionally rhizomatous. *Leaves basal, ± linear*, often arranged in two ranks or rosulate. Inflorescence an *umbel of regular flowers*, subtended by 2–8 involucral bracts, often reduced to a few flowers or to a solitary flower. Fruit a fleshy berry or longitudinally dehiscing capsule.

ANACARDIACEAE Mango Family
Trees, shrubs, occasionally suffrutices, *dioecious (with male and female flowers on separate trees)* but sometimes with bisexual flowers. Leaves compound, either pinnately or with *3 leaflets*, without stipules. Fruit an aggregate of fleshy, edible berries.

APIACEAE (Umbelliferae) Carrot Family
Annual or perennial herbs, *often aromatic*, with hollow internodes, often with tuberous rootstock, occasionally shrubs or trees. Leaves usually alternate, rarely opposite, usually *much divided*, with a sheathing petiole, without stipules. Inflorescence generally a simple or compound *umbel*.

APOCYNACEAE (including Asclepiadaceae and Periplocaceae) Oleander Family
Trees, erect or scandent shrubs, shrublets, subshrubs, lianas, perennial, rarely annual herbs, often succulent, with *milky or clear*

sap. Leaves simple, opposite or in whorls and rarely with stipules. Inflorescence mostly a cyme with the oldest flower usually at the top, sometimes racemose or umbelliform. Flowers bisexual, regular, small to large, showy, *fragrant*, occasionally with an obnoxious smell. *Corona of 5 or more, free or fused lobes*. Fruit a berry, drupe, samara or a pair (often 1 by abortion) of ventrally dehiscent follicular or baccate mericarps. Four subfamilies are represented in this book: Subfamily Apocynoideae, Subfamily Plumerioideae, Subfamily Periplocoideae and Subfamily Asclepiadoideae.

ARACEAE   Arum Lily Family
Perennial herbs, rarely shrublets, erect or climbing, usually monoecious or dioecious. Inflorescence with an *outer funnel-shaped spathe enclosing a finger-like, stalkless spadix* with a male and female zone.

ASPARAGACEAE   Asparagus Family
Suffrutices or climbers with perennial or annual stems from a compact, woody base; roots fibrous or often tuberous. Leaves *small and reduced to scales or spines*. Cladodes solitary or fascicled, persistent, flat, linear to ovate. Flowers *star-like*, usually *white or cream-coloured, fragrant*. Fruit a fleshy berry.

ASPHODELACEAE   (previously under Liliaceae) Asphodel Family
Succulent perennials with a rhizome or a stem. Leaves usually toothed, often arranged in basal rosettes. *Perianth segments 3 + 3*, free or nearly free or fused into a tube. Fruit a 3-locular, dry, loculicidal capsule.

ASTERACEAE   (Compositae) Daisy Family
Annual or perennial herbs, shrublets and shrubs, occasionally trees. Leaves usually alternate, rarely opposite, often in a basal rosette. Inflorescence comprising a capitulum (flowerhead) surrounded by an involucre of bracts. Flowers of two types: *strap-like ray-florets and tubular disc-florets*. Fruit crowned with a white tuft of hair, the pappus.

BALSAMINACEAE   Balsam Family
Soft, *succulent* herbs, often with *watery, translucent stems*, usually growing in *damp, shady places*. Leaves opposite or alternate, toothed. Flowers bisexual, irregular. Sepals usually 3, free, posterior one petaloid and *usually spurred*.

BEGONIACEAE   Begonia Family
Monoecious herbs or undershrubs, mostly *fleshy*, with stems *swollen at the nodes*, with membranous stipules. Leaves alternate, generally *asymmetrical*, palmately veined, margins entire, toothed, lobed or dissected. Flowers unisexual, regular or irregular, showy.

BIGNONIACEAE   Bignonia Family
Trees, shrubs, some scrambling, or climbers, rarely herbs, rarely spiny. Leaves usually compound, opposite in four rows along the stem, the pairs alternating at right angles, without stipules. Flowers showy, *bell- or funnel-shaped*, clustered in cymose arrangement with the oldest flowers at the top.

BORAGINACEAE Borage Family
Annual or perennial herbs, shrubs or trees, rarely climbers, *variably hairy throughout*; hairs often with *conspicuous multicellular bases*. Leaves alternate, without stipules. Inflorescence consisting of 1 or more determinate *coiled cymes* which uncoil progressively as the flowers open.

BRASSICACEAE (Cruciferae) Mustard Family
Annual, biennial or perennial *herbs*, suffrutices and shrubs, glabrous or hairy. Leaves mostly alternate, often crowded in a basal rosette. Flowers bisexual, usually regular. Fruit a *capsule*, usually dehiscing by 2 valves (*the rim often remaining behind*).

BUDDLEJACEAE (previously included in Loganiaceae)
Shrubs, trees or subshrubs; pubescence often scaly or stellate. Leaves opposite or occasionally subopposite, alternate or ternate, stipules present or represented by an interpetiolar ridge. Flowers regular, bisexual, usually in many-flowered, terminal or axillary, paniculate cymes. Fruit a small, ovoid, obovoid or oblong capsule.

CAMPANULACEAE Canterbury-bell Family
Herbs, undershrubs or small shrubs, often with milky juice. Leaves alternate, simple, entire, toothed, lobed or cut, without stipules. Flowers regular; calyx tube united with the ovary; corolla tube *bell-shaped*.

CAPPARACEAE Caper Family
Herbs, *shrubs or trees*, sometimes scandent. Leaves alternate, simple or 3–5-foliolate. Petals 4, free, often stalked. Stamens conspicuous, 4–*many*. Fruit a *long, narrow capsule* opening by 2 valves or a berry.

CARYOPHYLLACEAE Carnation Family
Annual or perennial *herbs*, or subshrubs, rarely shrubs, often with branches forked, in one or more pairs. Leaves generally opposite; stem nodes swollen, and the bases of each leaf pair often joining them. Petals 5, free, tips often deeply cleft.

CLUSIACEAE (Guttiferae) Mangosteen Family
Trees, shrubs or herbs, with resinous juice. Leaves opposite, subopposite or whorled, simple, entire. *Stamens many, free*.

COLCHICACEAE (previously included in Liliaceae)
Erect or climbing geophytes; with subterranean, starch-rich corms to tubers, sometimes stoloniferous. Leaves few and basally concentrated, sheathing at base, parallel-veined. Perianth 3 + 3.

COMMELINACEAE Commelina Family
Perennials or annuals, or occasionally rhizomatous or stoloniferous herbs, often somewhat succulent, rarely aquatic. Flowers bisexual or bisexual and male, regular or irregular, often with blue or yellow petals, *borne in spathes* (boat-shaped bracts). Fruit a 2- or 3-valved capsule.

CONVOLVULACEAE Morning-glory Family
Herbs or shrubs, frequently *twining*, one genus totally parasitic (*Cuscuta* or dodder). Leaves alternate, often lobed or ± heart-shaped. Flowers *funnel-shaped*, often subtended by 2 or more bracts. Fruit a 4-seeded capsule.

CRASSULACEAE Tacky Family
Herbs, undershrubs or shrubs, often *fleshy and succulent*. Leaves mostly entire, often in basal rosettes. Flowers bisexual, regular, small but massed in showy corymbs or panicles. Fruit usually a head of free follicles often enclosed by dry petals.

CUCURBITACEAE Pumpkin Family
Monoecious or dioecious herbs, shrubs or undershrubs, *prostrate or climbing*, sometimes with a tuberous or woody rootstock. Stems often *climbing by means of spirally coiled tendrils*. Leaves alternate, usually palmately veined, often palmately lobed. Flowers usually unisexual, usually white or yellow. Fruit are berries, varying in size and shape, with hard or leathery walls, sometimes covered with *spiny processes*, sometimes poisonous.

DIPSACACEAE Teasel or Scabious Family
Annual or perennial herbs or shrublets, glabrous or variously hairy. Leaves opposite, mainly in a *basal rosette*. Flowers bisexual, irregular, aggregated into dense, cymose heads (capitula) subtended by involucral bracts, often with *longer marginal flowers*. Fruit a dry cypsela.

ERICACEAE Erica Family
Shrublets, shrubs or occasionally small trees. Leaves *many, small*, firm, usually *linear*, mostly whorled, sometimes alternate or spirally arranged. Petals 5, united to form a short to *conspicuous tube*. Anthers opening by means of pores and often ornamented with outgrowths.

ERIOSPERMACEAE (previously under Liliaceae)
Perennial herbs, small to medium-sized, with single to multiple globose or irregularly shaped tuber or proliferation of rhizomes or stolons. Leaves 1–several, basally concentrated. Inflorescence a few–many-flowered simple raceme. Tepals 3 + 3.

EUPHORBIACEAE Euphorbia or Rubber Family
Herbs, shrubs, trees, *sometimes succulent*, sometimes twining or climbing, monoecious or dioecious; *latex often present, milky, sometimes watery*. The genera have characteristic *cup-shaped* inflorescences known as cyathia, in which several very reduced male flowers and a single female flower are usually found. Fruit usually a *3-locular* capsule.

FABACEAE (Leguminosae) Bean or Pod-bearing Family
Trees, shrubs, climbers, lianas or herbs. Leaves usually alternate, often pinnate or pinnately *3-foliolate* or digitately compound, occasionally 1-foliolate; *stipules usually present*. Flowers various. Fruit generally a 2-valved, dehiscent *pod*. Divided into three

subfamilies, namely Mimosoideae (*woody plants* often *armed with prickles*; inflorescence a *spike-like or globose head*), Caesalpinioideae (woody shrubs and shrublets; leaves pinnately compound or *deeply 2-lobed*; flowers irregular, usually showy) and Papilionoideae (herbaceous or woody plants; leaves simple or variously compound; flowers sweet-pea-shaped, made up of 5 unequal petals with the upper one a large, conspicuous *standard*, the two side ones small and with *stalked wings*, and the two basal ones united into a boat-shaped structure, the *keel*).

GENTIANACEAE   Gentian Family
Annual, biennial or perennial, terrestrial or occasionally *aquatic herbs*. Leaves mostly opposite, sometimes in verticils. Flowers bisexual, rarely unisexual, regular. Petals 4 or 5, united, often *twisted in bud*. Fruit a capsule, dehiscing septicidally.

GERANIACEAE   Geranium Family
Herbs, geophytes, subshrubs or shrubs; stems often with jointed nodes; usually *aromatic*. Leaves opposite or alternate, usually lobed, often palmately or pinnately dissected or compound; stipules usually present. Fruit a characteristic *beaked, dehiscent capsule*, opening spontaneously when ripe and breaking up into portions called mericarps.

GESNERIACEA   Gloxinia and Streptocarpus Family
Annual, perennial or monocarpic (blooming and fruiting only once and then dying) herbs, usually *stemless*, usually found in *moist or shady places*. Leaves solitary or few or rosulate, *often basal*. Flowers often solitary, borne on *long, slender stalks*. Petals 5, fused into a *basal tube*, the free ends being oblique. Fruit a many-seeded capsule.

GUNNERACEAE   Gunnera Family
Perennial herbs, nearly stemless, mainly rhizomatous; monoecious or flowers bisexual. Leaves radical, alternate, simple, long-stalked, entire, lobed or crenate. Flowers small, in *compound spikes*, sometimes with male flowers towards tip and female at base. Fruit a fleshy or leathery drupe.

HYACINTHACEAE   (previously under Liliaceae) Hyacinth Family
Perennial, bulbous herbs; *bulbs* generally with a membranous outer tunic and a number of bulb scales. Leaves 1–many, basal, usually *contemporary with the flowers*, in a rosette. Perianth segments free or sometimes fused at the base.

HYPOXIDACEAE   Star Lily Family
Herbaceous geophytes, with vertical rhizomes or fibrous corms, often pubescent with compound hairs. Leaves 1–many, basal, often containing raphides (needle-shaped crystals of calcium oxalate). Flowers showy, *star-like, yellow*, orange, pink or *white*, often green-backed, borne on an axillary, leafless, usually hairy stalk.

ILLECEBRACEAE   (sometimes included under Caryophyllaceae)
Annual or perennial herbs, rarely shrublets. Leaves opposite, often with *membranous stipules*. Flowers bisexual, small, regular, green or white. Petals absent. Fruit a nutlet.

IRIDACEAE   Iris Family

Perennial, evergreen or deciduous herbs. Rootstock a rhizome or corm. Leaves *sword-shaped* and arranged in 2 ranks. Inflorescence generally a *spike*. Perianth showy with 3 + 3 segments, often united below into a tube.

LAMIACEAE (Labiatae)   Sage Family

Herbs, mainly perennial, shrubs or trees, often *aromatic*; branches *usually 4-angled*. Leaves opposite or whorled, margins entire, toothed or sometimes lobed. Flowers usually irregular, often *2-lipped*, solitary and opposite or aggregated into cymes or whorls arranged in terminal spikes, racemes or panicles.

LENTIBULARIACEAE   Bladderwort Family

Carnivorous, perennial or annual *herbs, aquatic or terrestrial in moist places*. Leaves simple, entire or much divided, rosulate or scattered on stolons, some modified into *bladder- or bottle-like pitchers (traps) for catching small organisms*. Flowers bisexual, irregular, 2-lipped and spurred.

LILIACEAE   Lily Family

Erect herbs with *scaly bulb*. Leaves alternate, distributed along stem, sessile, flat, *parallel-veined*. Flowers bisexual, regular, often solitary, but up to 7 in a raceme. Tepals 3 + 3.

LINACEAE   Flax Family

Herbs or undershrubs, rarely shrublets or small trees. Leaves alternate, small, entire and with or without stipules. Flowers regular, bisexual, in panicles or cymes. Fruit a globose, septicidal capsule, or drupe.

LOBELIACEAE   Lobelia Family

Herbs, shrublets, rarely entirely woody, often with milky juice; often found in *moist places*. Leaves alternate, sometimes radical, opposite or whorled, simple, without stipules. Flowers *showy*, irregular, often *2-lipped*, inverted on their axis through 180°.

LORANTHACEAE   Lighted Candles Family

Mainly shrubby, brittle, perennial, *aerial hemiparasites* of other dicotyledons, often with swollen nodes. Leaves opposite, semi-opposite, alternate or whorled, simple, entire, predominantly evergreen. Flowers usually large, tubular brightly coloured with yellows and reds, mostly opening explosively. Calyx reduced to a low rim, the calyculus. Fruit usually a 1-seeded berry, with a viscous layer.

MALPIGHIACEAE   Barbados Cherry Family

Perennial scramblers, climbers, shrubs, or rarely shrublets, often covered with *T-shaped hairs*. Leaves usually opposite, glands often present on either the leaf stalk or the lower surface of the blade. Flowers bisexual, usually regular. Fruit breaking up into 2 or 3 one-seeded, winged mericarps, each with a dorsal or lateral *wing*.

MALVACEAE   Cotton Family

Herbs, shrubs or trees, usually with *star-shaped hairs*, sometimes prickly or with small scales. Leaves alternate, simple or often variously lobed, palmately veined. Calyx usually subtended by an *epicalyx*. Stamens numerous, *united into a tube around the style*, joined to the petals at the base.

MELASTOMATACEAE   Wild Rose-apple Family

Herbs, shrubs or trees, rarely climbing or prostrate; *stems 4-angled*. Leaves opposite and at right angles to the next, often with 3–9 prominent parallel veins. Flowers showy, regular, bisexual. Stamen filaments *elbow-shaped*, with sterile appendages of various shapes. Fruit a loculicidal capsule or berry.

MENYANTHACEAE

Perennial or annual *aquatic or wetland herbs*, with tufted rootstocks or horizontal creeping rhizomes. Leaves alternate, with sheathing petiole, simple, linear to orbicular. Petals 5, united at the base, yellow, white or pink, usually with *hairs or crests* on the inside. Fruit a capsule.

MESEMBRYANTHEMACEAE   Midday-flower Family

Annual to perennial *succulents*, ranging from small to compact and tufted to prostrate to decumbent; herbs, dwarf shrubs, subshrubs or shrubs, rarely spiny. Leaves opposite, rarely alternate. Flowers bisexual, regular; petals *many, free* or shortly connate at base. Fruit a *loculicidal capsule*, splitting open when dry, or mostly when wetted, by means of hygroscopic expanding keels.

MOLLUGINACEAE   Mollugo Family

Annual or perennial herbs or subshrubs, scarcely or nonsucculent. Leaves alternate, rarely opposite, often crowded into *basal rosettes*. Flowers bisexual, regular, mostly *inconspicuous*, usually greenish white, sometimes pink or red.

NYCTAGINACEAE   Four-o'clock Family

Annual or perennial herbs, shrubs, climbers or trees; stems frequently swollen at nodes, sometimes spiny. Leaves usually opposite, sometimes alternate, simple, entire. Flowers bisexual, regular, often brightly coloured. Fruit an achene or thin-walled nutlet.

NYMPHAEACEAE   Waterlily Family

Aquatic, rhizomatous, perennial herbs rooted in bottom mud. Leaves spirally arranged on rhizome, usually round or oval, cordate, *floating*. Flowers, regular, bisexual, solitary, usually large, *showy*, often scented. Stamens *numerous*, spirally arranged. Fruit a large, fleshy or spongy berry.

OLEACEAE   Olive and Jasmine Family

Trees, shrubs, climbers or occasionally low, woody-based, herbaceous plants. Leaves opposite, simple or compound. Flowers regular, bisexual; petals 4- or more-lobed, often forming a long or short tube.

ONAGRACEAE   Evening Primrose Family

Annual, biennial or perennial herbs, sometimes aquatic. Leaves opposite or alternate, simple, entire, or variously lobed. Flowers bisexual, mostly solitary and axillary, subtending leaves; petals 4 or 5, free, caducous. Fruit a capsule or nut, often elongated; seeds smooth or papillose.

ORCHIDACEAE   Orchid Family

Perennial herbs, terrestrial, epiphytic or saprophytic; with underground root tubers, corms, rhizomes, or above-ground pseudobulbs. Leaves cauline or basal, alternate, often distichous, rarely opposite. Sepals 3, mostly coloured and petaloid, median one often spurred; petals (lateral inner perianth lobes) 2, rather simple. *Lip* (median inner perianth lobe) often lobed and spurred, usually facing down.

OXALIDACEAE   Sorrel Family

Stemless or caulescent herbs, mostly with *bulbs*, sometimes with contractile roots. Leaves alternate or basal, palmately or pinnately compound, rarely 1-foliolate; leaflets often folded together at night. Flowers bisexual, regular, mostly solitary, in umbels or racemes. Fruit a *5-lobed capsule*, ejecting seeds explosively.

PAPAVERACEAE   Poppy Family

Annual, biennial or perennial *herbs*, sometimes prickly, with a clear white, yellow or orange-coloured, often sticky latex. Leaves alternate, basal and/or cauline, entire to much divided. Flowers bisexual, regular, usually *solitary on long stalks*. Fruit a capsule opening by *pores or slits*.

PASSIFLORACEAE   Passion-flower or Granadilla Family

Annual or perennial herbs, shrubs, small trees or climbers, often with *large, tuber-like stems*, often furnished with axillary *tendrils*. Leaves alternate, simple or compound, usually palmately lobed, with small, often deciduous stipules. Flowers bisexual or unisexual, regular, mostly solitary; *corona* often present, comprising thread-like processes or scales. Fruit a loculicidally 3–5-valved capsule or a berry.

PEDALIACEAE   Sesame Family

Annual or perennial *herbs*, sometimes with a short, swollen stem and tuberous roots, rarely shrubs or small trees, *sometimes spiny*. Petals 5, united into a tube. Fruit a capsule or nut, *often horned or with spines*.

PHYTOLACCACEAE   Pokeweed Family

Herbs, shrubs, or small trees, sometimes scrambling, often somewhat succulent. Leaves alternate, simple, entire. Flowers small, regular, bisexual (unisexual in few members of *Phytolacca*; plants then usually dioecious). Fruit fleshy or dry berries.

PLANTAGINACEAE   Plantago Family

Annual or perennial herbs. Leaves simple, usually all in a basal rosette or sometimes cauline, spirally arranged, *venation parallel*, without stipules. Flowers bisexual, regular in a dense or lax *spike* on a very *long, leafless stalk*. Fruit a circumscissile capsule.

PLUMBAGINACEAE   Plumbago Family

Shrubs, lianas, or herbs. Leaves alternate, simple, entire to lobed. Flowers bisexual, regular; sepals fused into a cylindrical tube, ribbed, often with *glandular hairs*; petals 5, *fused into a tube*. Fruit a dry, membranous, 1-seeded achene.

POLYGALACEAE   Milkwort Family

Herbs, shrubs, undershrubs or small trees. Leaves alternate, sometimes fascicled, rarely opposite, simple, entire. Flowers bisexual, irregular, superficially resembling flowers of papilionaceous Fabaceae; sepals 5, inner two wing-like and petal-like; petals ± reduced, 3–5, one often with a brush-like appendage.

POLYGONACEAE   Rhubarb Family

Annual or perennial herbs, shrubs or climbers, sometimes monoecious; stems often with *swollen nodes*. Many species found in *moist places* such as along streams, irrigation furrows and watercourses. Stipules usually conspicuous and united with base of petiole to form a tubular, persistent or deciduous, membranous to hyaline, often *bilobed or fringed sheath* (*ocrea*), or sometimes reduced or absent. Fruit a *trigonous or lenticular nut*, enclosed by the persistent membranous sepals.

PORTULACACEAE   Purslane Family

Annual, biennial or perennial herbs, sometimes with thickened, ± woody, short basal stems, occasionally soft-wooded shrubs or undershrubs, rarely small trees, often with most parts *succulent*. Leaves opposite or alternate. Flowers bisexual or occasionally unisexual, regular; petals 4–6, free. Stamens as many as the petals. Fruit a capsule, opening by means of valves or a *lid*.

RANUNCULACEAE   Buttercup Family

Perennial, rarely annual or biennial herbs, sometimes shrubby or climbing. Leaves alternate or opposite, often in a basal rosette, compound with bases forming a sheath. Fruit an aggregate of achenes, sometimes crowned with *plumed styles*.

ROSACEAE   Rose Family

Deciduous or evergreen trees, shrubs or herbs, usually perennial, erect, scandent or prostrate, sometimes stems and leaves armed with *prickles or thorns*. Petals 5, free. Stamens *many*, free.

RUBIACEAE   Gardenia Family

Trees, shrubs, annual or perennial herbs, sometimes spiny or prickly. Leaves opposite or whorled, with *interpetiolar stipules*, sometimes leaf-like. Petals 4 or 5, united into a tube; mouth of tube usually hairy. Fruit a capsule, berry or drupe, *crowned with persistent calyx lobes*.

SANTALACEAE   Sandalwood Family

Trees, shrubs, *herbs*, often *hemiparasitic on roots of other plants*. Leaves alternate or opposite, simple, entire, often bluish green, often reduced to scales. Flowers *small, often white or greenish*. Fruit indehiscent, a dry or fleshy nut or drupe.

SCROPHULARIACEAE   Snapdragon Family

Annual or perennial, terrestrial, amphibious or aquatic *herbs*, sometimes undershrubs, rarely shrubs or small trees. Leaves opposite, without stipules. Flowers often *2-lipped*; petals 4 or 5, united. Stamens 4, two of which are longer than the others. Fruit a many-seeded capsule.

SOLANACEAE   Potato Family

Herbs, shrubs, erect or climbing, rarely trees, occasionally spiny with *yellow spines*. Leaves alternate, often *strong-smelling when crushed*. Flowers bisexual, regular or slightly irregular, *star-shaped*, often purple. Petals 5, united; stamens often *bright yellow*. Fruit a many-seeded berry or prickly capsule.

STERCULIACEAE   Star-chestnut Family

Trees, shrubs, undershrubs or herbs, usually with *star-shaped hairs*. Leaves alternate, often *palmately lobed*, with stipules. Petals 5, free, twisted in bud. Fruit a dehiscent or indehiscent capsule.

THYMELAEACEAE   Gonna Family

Shrubs, shrublets or small trees, often *ericoid*, rarely perennial herbs; stems and branches with tough, cortical, often shining *fibres*. Leaves alternate or opposite, sessile or shortly stalked, needle-like, 1-nerved, to flat. Flowers bisexual, regular, long and tubular, often in dense terminal *heads*.

TILIACEAE   Linden Family

Annual or perennial herbs, shrubs, or small trees, often with *star-shaped hairs*. Leaves alternate, in two ranks, usually *asymmetrical*. Stamens *many, free, often borne on a short column*.

TURNERACEAE   Wormskioldia Family

Herbs, shrublets or shrubs, usually pubescent. Leaves alternate, simple, variously incised or entire, sometimes with conspicuous glands or extrafloral nectaries. Flowers bisexual, regular; petals 5, free, stalked, twisted in bud. Fruit a capsule with 3 valves.

VAHLIACEAE

Annual or perennial herbs or *subshrubs*, dichotomously branched, glabrous or pubescent with multicellular, often *gland-tipped hairs*. Leaves opposite, sessile to subsessile, simple, ovate to linear, entire. Flowers bisexual, regular, *white or yellow*.

VELLOZIACEAE   Vellozia Family

Fibrous perennials with dwarf and tufted stems covered with numerous leaf bases. Leaves *linear*, spirally arranged, crowded at ends of stems. Flowers bisexual, regular, showy. Perianth segments 3 + 3, petaloid.

VERBENACEAE   Verbena Family

Herbs, shrubs or small trees, with branches often *4-angled*, sometimes spinescent. Leaves opposite, often *strongly aromatic*.

Flowers bisexual, often *2-lipped*, in spikes, racemes or corymbs. Fruit a drupe with 2 or 4 pyrenes or dividing at maturity into 2 or 4 nutlets or pyrenes.

VIOLACEAE   Violet Family
Perennial, rarely annual, herbs, shrublets, shrubs or trees. Leaves alternate, rarely opposite, simple; stipules 2, leaf-like, small or minute, persistent or caducous. Flowers bisexual, irregular; petals 5, free.

VISCACEAE   Mistletoe Family
Shrubby, monoecious or dioecious, brittle, glabrous, hemiparasitic, *aerial parasites* on dicotyledons; *nodes articulated, often swollen*. Leaves opposite, simple, entire, sometimes *reduced to scales*. Flowers unisexual, minute, yellow or greenish, solitary or clustered with 3 or 4, free, valvate often much-reduced perianth segments. Fruit a 1-seeded berry or drupe, with a *sticky inner layer*.

XYRIDACEAE
Perennial, rarely annual, tufted, *grass-like*, usually *marsh herbs*, with a compact, erect rhizome. Leaves radical, spirally arranged, narrowly ensiform, linear, terete or filiform, sheathing at base. Flowers bisexual, slightly irregular, 3-merous; petals *yellow*, rarely white or blue.

ZYGOPHYLLACEAE   Caltrop Family
Herbs, subshrubs or shrubs; branches often *jointed at nodes*. Leaves opposite or subopposite, rarely alternate or fascicled, often somewhat *fleshy*, simple, (1)2- or 3-foliolate or pinnate; leaflets sessile, opposite. Flowers bisexual, regular, solitary. Fruit a capsule, sometimes fleshy, often splitting into 5 indehiscent *mericarps*.

Notes

Illustrated guide

White/Cream-coloured Flowers

ARACEAE

Zantedeschia albomaculata subsp. ***albomaculata***

Kleinvarkblom

Robust, erect plant. Leaves large, heart-shaped. Inflorescence of outer funnel-shaped spathe, white to ivory to pale yellow, dark purple at the base on inside, enclosing a finger-like sessile spadix.

Ht: up to 50 cm.   **Fl:** Nov–Jan.
Distr: N, E, S.

COLCHICACEAE

Androcymbium melanthioides var. ***subulatum***

Pyjama Flower; Patrysblom

Small, perennial herb with short single stem just above ground from small corm. Leaves few, sheathing at base, broadly ovate tapering to narrow tip. Flowers small, green, ± 6 in heads hidden by broad, ovate, white, tinged pink bracts.

Ht: up to 20 cm. **Fl:** Jan–Mar. **Distr:** E, S.

ASPHODELACEAE

Trachyandra asperata var. ***swaziensis***
Wildeknoflok

Robust, erect geophyte with flowering-stem from short woody rootstock. Leaves many, wiry. Inflorescence widely branched, glandular-hairy. Flowers opening in late afternoon, white or pink with dark midrib and sometimes green spots.

Ht: up to 1 m.   **Fl:** Oct–Dec.   **Distr:** S, E.

Trachyandra margaretae

A hard, grass-like plant from small woody rhizome, growing in clumps. Leaves linear, ribbed, sparsely hairy to smooth. Inflorescence simple. Flowers white; ovary densely hairy.

Ht: up to 60 cm. **Fl**: Aug–Nov. **Distr**: N, E.

Kniphofia albescens

Robust, erect herb, perennial, usually growing in groups. Leaves ± 8, strongly keeled. Inflorescence a long-stalked, terminal, dense flowerhead. Flowers tubular, greenish white in bud, white or cream-coloured when mature.

Ht: up to 1 m.   **Fl**: Jan–Mar.   **Distr**: S, E.

ANTHERICACEAE

Chlorophytum angulicaule
(= *Anthericum angulicaule*)

Robust, perennial herb from stout, hard, woody, horizontal rhizome, covered with old leaf fibres. Leaves linear, ribbed, in 2 ranks, clasping at base. Flowers in groups of 3 or 4, white with dark keel.

Ht: 0.2–1.5 m.   **Fl**: Jun–Dec.   **Distr**: W, E.

Chlorophytum fasciculatum
(= *Anthericum fasciculatum*)

Erect, herbaceous perennial with horizontal woody rhizome covered with fibres from old leaf remains. Leaves linear to filiform. Inflorescence spike-like. Flowers white with green median stripes.

Ht: up to 60 cm. **Fl**: Oct–Mar. **Distr**: T.

Chlorophytum transvaalense
(= *Anthericum transvaalense*)

Robust, erect herb, perennial from woody rhizome covered with leaf-fibre remains. Leaves short, narrow, ribbed, hairy with long, white, spreading hairs. Flowers white with green stripes, opening in the morning, in unbranched many-flowered inflorescences.

Ht: up to 80 cm. **Fl**: Nov–Apr. **Distr**: T.

ALLIACEAE

Tulbaghia leucantha
Veld Onion

Tall, slender, erect, solitary or in groups, smelling of garlic when bruised. Leaves basal, linear. Inflorescence a long-stalked, few-flowered umbel. Flowers with cream-coloured tepals; corona orange.

Ht: up to 30 cm. **Fl**: Oct–Feb. **Distr**: T.

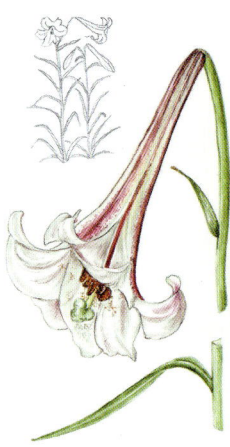

LILIACEAE

Lilium formosanum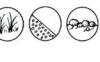
Lily

Robust, erect herb from perennial rootstock. Leaves lance-shaped, in whorls. Flowers 1–3, large, trumpet-shaped, white tinged with mauve, sweet-smelling, terminal.

Ht: up to 2 m. **Fl**: Jan–Mar. **Distr**: N, E.

HYACINTHACEAE

Albuca setosa

Robust, perennial herb with single pinkish flowering-stem from bulb with scales ending in mat of persistent fibres. Leaves ± 6, linear-lanceolate. Inflorescence a many-flowered raceme. Flowers white with broad green median stripe.

Ht: up to 40 cm. **Fl**: Sep–Feb. **Distr**: T.

Urginea sanguinea
Slangkop, Krimpsiekteblaar

Robust plant with flowering-stem from large bulb covered with red scales. Leaves not produced until after flowers. Inflorescence a terminal, many-flowered raceme. Flowering-stem lilac. Flowers small, white with brown median stripe.

Ht: up to 30 cm. **Fl**: Sep–Nov. **Distr**: T.

Scilla nervosa

Erect, herbaceous geophyte with tall flowering-stem from bulb covered with rows of fleshy scales. Leaves 6–8, erect, often twisted. Flowers white to greenish yellow, with blue anthers.

Ht: up to 40 cm. **Fl**: Nov–Jan. **Distr**: T.

Ornithogalum saundersiae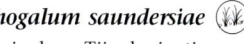
Chinkerinchee; Tjienkerientjee

Robust geophyte. Leaves broad, tapering to short point. Inflorescence a flat-topped raceme. Flowers creamy to white, without median stripe; ovary dark green to black.

Ht: up to 1 m. **Fl**: Jan–Mar. **Distr**: E.

Ornithogalum seineri

Slender, erect plant; bulb with firm outer tunic, forming short neck. Leaves ± 7, erect or spreading, channelled. Flowers faintly scented, white with broad green keel.

Ht: up to 40 cm. **Fl**: Oct–Feb. **Distr**: N, W, C, E.

Ornithogalum tenuifolium subsp. *tenuifolium*

Robust, erect flowering-stem from globose or ovoid bulb with thin tunic. Leaves ± 5, linear. Flowers small, white with broad green median stripe (turning red when dry), in compact terminal raceme.

Ht: up to 60 cm. **Fl**: Oct–Jan. **Distr**: N, C, E, S.

ASPARAGACEAE

Asparagus cooperi
Haakdoring

Robust, woody twiner or sometimes small shrublet, slightly zigzagging. Cladodes in clusters of 8, straight or recurved. Spines straight or recurved, at nodes. Flowers small, white, axillary or terminal.

Ht: up to 1 m. **Fl**: Apr–Nov. **Distr**: T.

Asparagus laricinus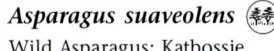

Erect, forming much-branched shrubs from fibrous roots, stems woody, white, hairy at first becoming smooth. Cladodes many, straight. Flowers white, axillary or terminal.

Ht: up to 2 m. **Fl**: Sep–Dec. **Distr**: W, C, E, S.

Asparagus suaveolens
Wild Asparagus; Katbossie

Erect shrublet, occasionally climbing or scrambling. Branches zigzagging, ending in sharp spine. Cladodes linear in groups of 3–6. Flowers small, star-shaped, white, streaked with purple. Fruit a globose, red or black, 1-seeded berry.

Ht: up to 1 m. **Fl**: throughout the year. **Distr**: T.

AMARYLLIDACEAE

Crinum lugardiae

Bulb large, globose, narrowed in neck. Leaves many, narrow, spreading at ground level, with undulate, ciliate margin. Inflorescence a 4–10-flowered umbel. Flowers tubular, curved, white with deep pink keel; anthers black; style rose.

Ht: up to 30 cm. **Fl:** Oct–Jan. **Distr:** N, W, C.

Pancratium tenuifolium

Slender, erect plant from bulb with tunic and neck. Leaves linear, slightly twisted. Flowers showy, 1–4 in umbel, long, tubular, funnel-shaped at mouth, white, opening at night; petals lobed.

Ht: up to 30 cm. **Fl:** Oct–Dec. **Distr:** N, C, E.

ORCHIDACEAE

Disperis fanniniae
Granny Bonnet; Moederkappie

Terrestrial with slender to stout flowering-stem. Leaves 3, cauline, cordate to lance-shaped, dark green above, purple below. Flowers white flushed pink or green, with conspicuous hood.

Ht: up to 45 cm. **Fl:** Jan–Apr. **Distr:** N, E, S.

Mystacidium capense

Short-stemmed epiphyte with many greyish roots, white-streaked. Leaves stiff, strap-shaped, unequally bilobed at tip. Flowers 6–12, white, widely spaced in several axillary inflorescences.

Fl: Sep–Jan. **Distr:** N, E.

LORANTHACEAE

Agelanthus natalitius subsp. ***zeyheri*** (formerly *Loranthus*)
Lighted Candles

Large parasitic shrub primarily on *Acacia* and *Combretum* trees. Leaves simple, opposite, ovate, hairy, deciduous. Flowers showy, tubular with swollen base, grey or white with yellow or orange lobes and yellow-green to red tips. Fruit a dark red ovoid berry.

Ht: up to 1 m. **Fl**: Oct–Feb. **Distr**: T.

SANTALACEAE

Thesium cytisoides

Small, erect root-parasite with much-branched stems from woody base forming bushes. Leaves small, narrow, linear. Flowers small, star-shaped, white, terminal.

Ht: up to 30 cm. **Fl**: Oct–Mar. **Distr**: T.

POLYGONACEAE

Oxygonum dregeanum subsp. ***canescens*** var. ***linearifolium***

Much-branched herb with annual, shortly hairy stems from perennial rootstock. Leaves linear, rarely with 1 or 2 short teeth at base of lower leaves. Flowers star-shaped, white with pinkish tinge.

Ht: up to 50 cm. **Fl**: Nov–Mar. **Distr**: C, S, E.

Oxygonum sinuatum

Annual, semi-erect to spreading herb. Ocrea fringed with reddish brown, ciliate, rigid seta. Leaves deeply lobed, red-rimmed. Flowers white with pinkish tinge, in lax thyrse of up to 3 flowers.

Ht: up to 40 cm. **Fl**: Nov–Mar. **Distr**: T.

AMARANTHACEAE
Aerva leucura

Robust, erect, much-branched, closely leafy herb or undershrub, shortly hairy throughout. Leaves obovate, margins undulate. Flowers small, white, silky hairy, in dense, terminal spikes in loose panicles.

Ht: up to 40 cm. **Fl**: Dec–Mar. **Distr**: T.

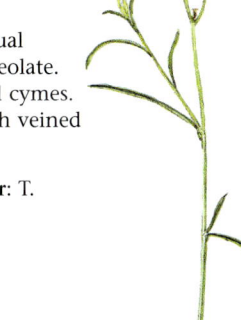

MOLLUGINACEAE

Limeum fenestratum
var. ***fenestratum***

Slender, erect, much-branched, annual herb. Leaves linear to narrowly lanceolate. Flowers small, white, in lax terminal cymes. Fruit round, a characteristic disc with veined membranous wings.

Ht: up to 20 cm. **Fl**: Nov–May. **Distr**: T.

ILLECEBRACEAE
Pollichia campestris

Erect, soft, much-branched undershrub. Leaves simple, linear, in whorls. Flowers small, crowded in sessile, axillary cymes surrounded by white, scarious bracts. Fruit an edible, fleshy, 1- or 2-seeded utricle.

Ht: up to 80 cm. **Fl**: Oct–May.
Distr: T.

CARYOPHYLLACEAE

Cerastium arabidis

Slender, erect, herbaceous perennial with little-branched, glandular-hairy stems. Leaves opposite, sessile, narrowly ovate. Flowers white, in terminal, few-flowered clusters.

Ht: up to 30 cm. **Fl**: Oct–Mar. **Distr**: T.

Silene undulata

Robust, erect, perennial herb, shortly hairy, with little-branched stems from woody base. Leaves opposite, ovate, margins wavy. Flowers white, terminal, long-stalked, with tubular green calyx.

Ht: up to 1.2 m. **Fl**: Oct–Apr. **Distr**: C, E.

RANUNCULACEAE

Knowltonia transvaalensis var. *transvaalensis*
Brandblare

Slender, erect, perennial herb. Leaves mostly basal, long-stalked, deeply 3-lobed; each lobe divided again, margins serrate. Flowers white, tinged with red, arranged in terminal umbels. Fruit an aggregation of small, fleshy berries.

Ht: up to 45 cm. **Fl**: Sep–May. **Distr**: N, E, S.

Clematis oweniae

Traveller's Joy; Klimop, Lemoenbloeisels

Climber with slender, spreading, hairy stems. Leaves with 7–9 widely spaced leaflets; each again divided, hairy. Flowers white, sweetly scented; stamens yellow, many in several rows.

Ht: up to 5 m. **Fl**: Feb–Apr, sometimes later. **Distr**: T.

(Often confused with *C. brachiata* for its similarity, but differs in having more rounded anthers in contrast to the more elongated anthers of *C. brachiata*.)

CAPPARACEAE

Cleome monophylla

Single-leaved Cleome, Spindlepod, Spider Flower

Erect, annual herb with branched, hairy stems, often glandular-hairy. Leaves usually simple. Flowers pink to pale mauve with transverse yellow band outlined in purple on upper two petals. Fruit a linear capsule.

Ht: up to 50 cm. **Fl**: Nov–Mar. **Distr**: T.

CRASSULACEAE

Crassula capitella subsp. ***nodulosa***

Perennial, rarely biennial with 2–several basal rosettes, with leaf pairs spirally arranged. Leaves obovate, with stout marginal cilia. Inflorescence a spike-like, unbranched thyrse. Flowers tubular, white, cream-coloured or tinged pink.

Ht: up to 40 cm. **Fl**: Jan–Apr. **Distr**: T.

Crassula capitella subsp. *sessilicymula*

Similar to subsp. *nodulosa* but differs in its branched inflorescence, lance-shaped leaves and different habitat.

Distr: C.

Crassula setulosa var. *setulosa*

Perennial with slender, erect, hairy stems. Basal leaves in a rosette, broadly elliptic; upper leaves sessile, opposite, hairy. Inflorescence a round-topped thyrse, many-flowered. Flowers tubular, white, often tinged red.

Ht: up to 25 cm. **Fl**: Feb–Apr. **Distr**: T.

FABACEAE

Melilotus alba

Sweet Clover, Bokhara Clover; Witstinkklawer

Slender, erect, much-branched herb. Leaves long-stalked, 3-foliolate; leaflets ovate, finely serrate at apex. Flowers small, white, in dense axillary, long-stalked inflorescences.

Ht: up to 1 m. **Fl**: Sep–Mar. **Distr**: T.

Indigofera zeyheri

Tall, slender, erect herb, much-branched. Leaves compound, with 3–7 pairs of opposite leaflets and a terminal one, shortly hairy. Inflorescence axillary, long-stalked. Flowers small, white with reddish standard.

Ht: up to 1 m. **Fl**: Nov–Feb. **Distr**: W, C, E, S.

Abrus precatorius subsp. ***africanus***

Lucky Bean, Crab's Eyes, Coral-bead Plant, Rosary Pea

Robust twiner in other plants. Leaves compound, with up to 10 pairs of opposite, grey-green, ovate leaflets and a terminal one. Flowers white, yellow, pink or mauve. Pods hairy, densely clustered, with many bright red, shiny seeds with a black spot.

Fl: Oct–Dec. **Distr**: N, C, E.

GERANIACEAE

Geranium wakkerstroomianum

Diffuse, perennial herb with straggling, loosely branched white-hairy stems. Stipules deeply divided. Leaves digitately 5-lobed ± two-thirds to base. Flowers with deeply notched petals, white, veined pink or red, rarely pink.

Fl: Oct–Feb, sometimes later. **Distr**: N, E.

Monsonia angustifolia

White flower-colour form. See p. 79.

Monsonia glauca

Dysentery Herb; Geitabossie, Keitabossie, Naaldebossie

Erect, decumbent or prostrate herb. Leaves alternate at base, long-ovate, slender-stalked, toothed. Inflorescence lateral, axillary, 1–3-flowered. Flowers white or creamy.

Ht: up to 50 cm. **Fl**: Oct–May. **Distr**: N, E.

Pelargonium alchemilloides

Perennial, leafy herb with decumbent, hairy stems from tuberous rootstock. Leaves 5–7-lobed; lobes irregularly toothed. Inflorescences 3–5 together, sometimes up to 15-flowered umbels. Flowers white or cream-coloured or pink, rarely with pink or red markings.

Ht: up to 30 cm. **Fl**: Oct–Dec.
Distr: N, E, S, W.

Pelargonium dolomiticum

Perennial herb, much-branched subshrub with long, slender branches dying back in winter. Leaves irregularly deeply divided, densely glandular-hairy, margins sometimes red-rimmed. Flowers white, cream-coloured, pink or light purple with red to dark red markings at base; claws of spathulate petals folded lengthwise, appearing tubular.

Ht: up to 50 cm. **Fl**: Aug–May.
Distr: N, W, C, S.

POLYGALACEAE

Polygala albida

Erect, annual herb with slender, hairy stems. Leaves narrowly elliptic. Flowers white, greenish white or pale pink, in dense terminal clusters.

Ht: up to 60 cm. **Fl**: Dec–May. **Distr**: T.

EUPHORBIACEAE

Clutia monticola var. *monticola*

Robust, erect shrublet with several smooth stems from woody rootstock. Leaves sessile, ovate, pale green, turning pink or salmon-coloured with age. Flowers small, greenish white, hidden by leaves.

Ht: up to 50 cm. **Fl**: Jul–Dec.
Distr: N, W, C, E.

ANACARDIACEAE

Lannea edulis var. *edulis*

Erect shrublet with strong underground rootstock from which stems and short branches develop annually. Leaves with 2–4 pairs of ovate leaflets, velvety. Flowers appearing before the leaves, cream-coloured with red calyx. Fruit fleshy, red.

Ht: up to 50 cm. **Fl**: Sep–Oct. **Distr**: T.

MALVACEAE

Sida ternata

Slender, erect shrublet. Leaves long-stalked, divided into 3–5 lobes, margins irregularly toothed. Flowers white, solitary, on long slender stalks.

Ht: up to 60 cm. **Fl**: Oct–Apr. **Distr**: T.

Hibiscus trionum

Black-eyed Susan, Bladder Hibiscus, Bladderweed; Terblansbossie, Uurblom

Erect or semi-erect, annual herb with white-bristly hairy stems. Leaves deeply 3-lobed with the middle lobe the longest; lobes further divided. Flowers solitary, cream-coloured to yellow with deep purple centre. Fruit enclosed in bladdery calyces.

Ht: up to 1.5 m. **Fl**: Nov–Mar. **Distr**: T.

PASSIFLORACEAE

Basananthe sandersonii

Perennial herb with slender, smooth stems from woody rootstock. Tendrils sometimes present. Leaves sessile, lance-shaped, grey-green, sharp-pointed. Flowers white, in 1–3-flowered axillary inflorescences.

Ht: up to 60 cm. **Fl:** Sep–Oct. **Distr:** N, E.

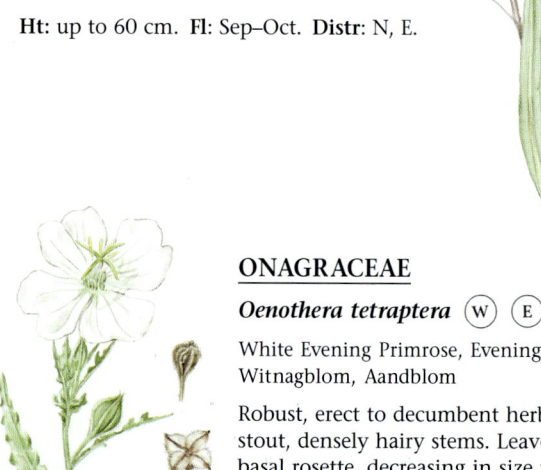

ONAGRACEAE

Oenothera tetraptera

White Evening Primrose, Evening Primrose; Witnagblom, Aandblom

Robust, erect to decumbent herb with stout, densely hairy stems. Leaves in a basal rosette, decreasing in size upwards, deeply lobed, or entire or shallowly toothed, densely hairy. Flowers solitary, axillary, white, fading to dark pink, opening at sunset. Fruit club-shaped, hairy.

Ht: up to 30 cm. **Fl:** Sep–Mar. **Distr:** T.

APIACEAE

Alepidea longifolia var. *longifolia*

Robust, erect, single-stemmed herb. Leaves mostly in a basal rosette; upper leaves stem-clasping, diminishing in size upwards, margins toothed, ending in a sharp point. Flowers small, in central clusters, surrounded by white, star-shaped bracts, in terminal umbels.

Ht: up to 1 m. **Fl:** Jan–May. **Distr:** N, E.

Berula erecta* subsp. *erecta

Water Parsnip, Toothache Root; Tandpynbossie

Robust, erect herb with perennial underground stems from which leaves arise. Leaves pinnately compound; leaflets ovate, toothed. Flowers small, greenish white or yellow, in branched terminal umbels.

Ht: up to 50 cm. **Fl**: Dec–Feb. **Distr**: T.

PLUMBAGINACEAE

Plumbago zeylanica

Straggling shrub. Leaves alternate, smooth, slightly scaly. Flowers tubular, with 5 white spreading lobes. Calyx gland-tipped, sticky to the touch.

Ht: up to 1.5 m. **Fl**: Mar–Apr. **Distr**: T.

OLEACEAE

Jasminum breviflorum

Climber, occasionally shrubby, with stems densely or sparsely hairy. Leaves simple, ovate, hairy or smooth. Inflorescence terminal, 3-flowered. Flowers tubular, white, fragrant; calyx shorter than tube. Fruit a globose berry, turning black when ripe.

Fl: Nov–Jan. **Distr**: N, W, C.

Jasminum fluminense

Woody climber or scrambler, sometimes small shrub. Leaves 3-foliolate; leaflets ovate, hairy on both surfaces. Flowers white, tubular, fragrant, terminal or axillary.

Fl: throughout the year. **Distr**: N, E.

BUDDLEJACEAE

Gomphostigma virgatum

Besembossie, Otterbossie

Erect, evergreen shrublet with long slender virgate branches. Leaves opposite with connecting ridge, single-veined. Flowers white, scented, in axils of upper leaves.

Ht: up to 2.6 m. **Fl**: Dec–Feb.
Distr: N, W, C, E.

APOCYNACEAE

Subfamily Plumerioideae

Ancylobotrys capensis (= *Landolphia capensis*)

Wild Apricot, Wild Peach; Wildeappelkoos, Wildeperske

Much-branched, scandent shrub or woody climber with milky latex. Leaves hairy on both surfaces when young, becoming smooth, dark green above, paler below. Flowers white, sweetly scented. Fruit globose, fleshy, apricot-coloured, with tough skin.

Ht: 1–2 m, sometimes up to 5 m.
Fl: Sep–Dec. **Distr**: N, W, C.

Subfamily Asclepiadoideae

Araujia sericifera

Moth Catcher, Bladder Flower; Motvanger, Melkbol

Robust, subwoody climber, with milky sap. Leaves opposite, ovate, dark green and smooth above, white and shortly hairy below. Flowers white or cream-coloured, tubular, axillary. Fruit large spongy capsules, ovoid, opening to release blackish seeds crowned with fine silky hairs.

Ht: up to 5 m or more. **Fl**: Dec–Feb.
Distr: C, S.

Pachycarpus schinzianus

Bitterwortel

Tall, robust, erect herb with milky sap. Leaves large, rough, wavy, red-rimmed. Flowers large, cup-shaped, white and green with purple markings, in terminal umbels.

Ht: up to 50 cm. **Fl**: Sep–Feb. **Distr**: T.

Gomphocarpus fruticosus

Cotton Milkbush, Milkweed; Blaasoppies, Gansies, Kapokmelkbossie

Robust, erect, much-branched herb or shrublet with slender branches, containing a milky sap. Flowers cream-coloured to yellow, up to 10 in pendulous umbels. Fruit inflated, beaked, hairy, with processes.

Ht: up to 1.2 m. **Fl**: Dec–Mar. **Distr**: T.

CONVOLVULACEAE

Convolvulus sagittatus

Wild Bindweed; Bobbejaantou, Rankbossie

Perennial with several slender, annual, prostrate or climbing stems from woody taproot. Leaves sagittate with linear central lobe, thinly hairy on both surfaces. Flowers funnel-shaped, white or pale pink.

Fl: Oct–Mar. **Distr**: T.

Ipomoea hochstetteri

Annual herbaceous climber, occasionally prostrate with long trailing stems. Leaves digitately compound, with 5 lobes. Inflorescence a 3–6-flowered cyme. Flowers funnel-shaped, with acute lobes, white or purplish mauve.

Fl: Feb–Mar. **Distr**: T.

BORAGINACEAE

Heliotropium steudneri

Erect perennial herb or dwarf shrub with much-branched, shortly rough-hairy stems from woody base. Leaves subsessile, lanceolate, alternate, margins wavy. Flowers small, tubular, white, in long terminal inflorescences, curling at tips with flowers on one side.

Ht: up to 50 cm. **Fl**: Sep–Mar. **Distr**: T.

Trichodesma physaloides

Chocolate Bells; Slangkop

Erect, branched, bushy, perennial herb with stems from woody rootstock. Older leaves with white spots on lower surface. Leaves opposite, ovate, sessile. Flowers bell-shaped, nodding, white; calyx dark pink to brown.

Ht: up to 50 cm. **Fl**: Aug–Oct. **Distr**: T.

VERBENACEAE

Lippia rehmannii

Rehmann Lippia; Beukesbossie, Laventelbos

Erect, much-branched, aromatic herb or small shrub with 4-angled roughly hairy stems. Leaves opposite, prominently veined, toothed, hairy, especially on veins. Flowers small, white, in axillary long-stalked elongated heads.

Ht: up to 60 cm. **Fl**: Oct–Mar. **Distr**: N, W, C, E.

Chascanum hederaceum var. *hederaceum*

Semi-erect herb with horizontal spreading stems from woody rootstock, shortly rough-hairy throughout. Leaves in pairs. Flowers tubular, 5-lobed, 2-lipped, cream-coloured or white.

Ht: up to 30 cm. **Fl**: Nov–Mar. **Distr**: T.

Chascanum incisum

Much-branched, perennial herb with spreading stems from woody rootstock, forming small bushes. Leaves opposite, long-stalked, deeply 5–7-lobed. Flowers tubular, 2-lipped, creamy white, in axillary spike.

Ht: up to 50 cm. **Fl**: Oct–Jan. **Distr**: T.

LAMIACEAE

Teucrium trifidum

Erect, soft undershrub with greyish hairy stems, branched from base. Leaves drying greyish green, deeply 3-lobed or 3–5-partite, rarely almost entire. Flowers tubular, white, in 3–7-flowered cyme.

Ht: up to 1.1 m. **Fl:** Nov–Feb. **Distr:** T.

Acrotome angustifolia

Erect, perennial herb with irregularly branched hairy stems from woody rootstock. Leaves narrow, linear-lanceolate, subsessile, toothed at apex. Flowers white, 2-lipped, in dense terminal flowerheads.

Ht: up to 1 m. **Fl:** Dec–Jun. **Distr:** N, W.

Acrotome hispida

Similar to *A. angustifolia* but leaves ovate. Flowers small, white or pale mauve, in 1 or 2 spaced rows.

Ht: up to 70 cm. **Fl:** Oct–Jun. **Distr:** C, S.

Leucas glabrata var. *glabrata*

Weak-stemmed, straggling, perennial herb, branched from woody rootstock, thinly hairy. Leaves subsessile, toothed. Inflorescence of several rows of 2–10-flowered clusters. Flowers tubular, white, densely hairy; calyx teeth ending in sharp point.

Ht: up to 80 cm. **Fl**: Sep–Nov.
Distr: N, C, E.

Stachys aethiopica

Perennial herb with little-branched, shortly hairy, decumbent stems. Leaves ovate, thinly hairy, margins toothed. Flowers tubular, white or pink to deep mauve with purple flecks on lower lip.

Ht: up to 50 cm. **Fl**: Jan–Mar.
Distr: E.

Satureja biflora

Erect herb with many closely leafy stems from woody, perennial rootstock, little-branched, hairy, bearded below the nodes. Leaves opposite, lemon-scented. Flowers in few–several-flowered axillary clusters, white or pale mauve; calyx ribbed, 5-toothed.

Ht: up to 60 cm. **Fl**: Aug–Dec. **Distr**: T.

Aeollanthus rehmannii

Perennial, semisucculent herb or subshrub with shortly hairy, spreading branches. Leaves fleshy, ovate, short, stiffly hairy below, margins toothed, often tinged reddish purple. Flowers white to pinkish mauve with reddish purple markings on upper lip, in branched inflorescences.

Ht: up to 50 cm. **Fl**: Dec–Apr. **Distr**: N, C, E, S.

Plectranthus grandidentatus

Perennial, semisucculent, strongly aromatic herb with trailing, densely white-woolly stems. Leaves long-stalked, softly succulent, ovate, deeply toothed. Inflorescence a lax terminal 3–6-flowered cyme. Flowers tubular, white, rarely purple, humped near calyx.

Fl: Feb–Apr. **Distr**: N, E.

Plectranthus laxiflorus

Tall, slender, erect, somewhat branched, thinly hairy, aromatic herb. Leaves stalked, ovate, red gland-dotted on undersurface. Flowers tubular, white or mauve with purple markings on the lower lip, slightly hairy.

Ht: up to 1.5 m. **Fl**: Oct–May. **Distr**: N, E.

Plectranthus rubropunctatus

Perennial herb or soft shrub with erect or procumbent, purplish, glandular-hairy stems. Leaves with red to brownish dots on undersurface. Flowers white, slightly flushed with pink, in sessile 3-flowered cymes.

Ht: up to 2 m. **Fl**: Jan–Jun. **Distr**: N, E.

Plectranthus verticillatus

Perennial, semisucculent herb with branched, procumbent stems. Leaves succulent, ovate to rotund, red gland-dotted below, margins toothed. Flowers tubular, white to pale mauve with mauve spots on upper lip, in sessile, 1–3-flowered cymes.

Fl: Jan–May. **Distr**: N, E.

Hemizygia albiflora

Much-branched, somewhat gnarled, woody shrublet with hairy, closely leafy stems. Leaves dark green on upper surface, densely white-hairy below. Inflorescence simple, with 4–6-flowered rows. Flowers tubular, white; stamens exserted.

Ht: up to 1.5 m. **Fl**: Dec–Apr. **Distr**: E.

Hemizygia canescens

Slender, erect, aromatic herb, woody at base, shortly grey-downy throughout. Leaves finely toothed. Inflorescence with pairs of branched, well-spaced flower clusters. Flowers tubular, the lips turned upwards and downwards, mauve or white; stamens and style exserted.

Ht: up to 60 cm. **Fl**: Jan–Apr. **Distr**: T.

Hemizygia persimilis

Tall, bushy, herb with many glandular-hairy stems from perennial, woody rootstock. Leaves subsessile, surfaces wrinkled, gland-dotted. Inflorescence simple, with rows of 2–6 flowers. Bracts ovate, white to rose-purple. Flowers tubular, white, drying yellow-brown.

Ht: up to 3 m. **Fl**: Sep–Dec. **Distr**: E.

Hemizygia pretoriae subsp. *pretoriae*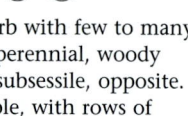

Erect, aromatic herb with few to many hairy stems from perennial, woody rootstock. Leaves subsessile, opposite. Inflorescence simple, with rows of 3–6 flowers. Flowers tubular, white to pale mauve.

Ht: up to 3 m. **Fl**: Sep–Mar. **Distr**: C, E.

Ocimum americanum var. *americanum*

Perennial herb or shrublet with much-branched, hairy stems from woody base. Leaves variable, hairy, gland-dotted below. Flowers lilac to mauve to white, in terminal rows.

Ht: up to 50 cm. **Fl**: Dec–May.
Distr: N, W, C, E.

Becium angustifolium

Erect, perennial herb or soft shrublet with hairy stems, branched in upper half. Leaves subsessile, aromatic, linear, grey-green, hairy, gland-dotted on both surfaces. Inflorescence slender, with 4–12 well-spaced rows of flowers. Flowers white; stamens exserted.

Ht: up to 60 cm. **Fl**: Oct–Apr.
Distr: N, C, W, S.

Becium filamentosum

Erect, perennial, soft shrub with hairy stems, branched in upper half. Leaves subsessile, smooth, gland-dotted below, hairy above. Inflorescence with 6–20 well-spaced rows of flowers. Flowers tubular, white to mauve.

Ht: up to 80 cm. **Fl**: Oct–Mar.
Distr: N, E.

Becium obovatum subsp. **obovatum** var. **galpinii**

Similar to var. *obovatum* but differs in having hairy leaves with conspicuous veins on undersurface and margins distinctly toothed.

Fl: Sep–Feb. **Distr**: W, E.

SOLANACEAE

Solanum tomentosum var. **coccineum** (W)

Kleingrysbitterappel(tjie), Slangappel(tjie)

Small, erect, spiny shrublet with much-branched stems from woody rootstock, grey-velvety hairy throughout. Leaves shallowly lobed, dark green above, paler below. Flowers star-shaped white, lilac or blue. Fruit small, globose, berries turning reddish when ripe.

Ht: up to 50 cm. **Fl**: Nov–Feb. **Distr**: T.

Solanum supinum

Small, much-branched shrub, densely spiny and white-woolly throughout. Leaves deeply divided almost to midrib. Flowers solitary, white; anthers yellow. Fruit a small, yellow, shiny, globose berry.

Ht: up to 30 cm. **Fl**: Nov–Dec. **Distr**: T.

SCROPHULARIACEAE

Zaluzianskya elongata

Slender, erect, herb with annual, thinly hairy, gland-dotted stems from woody rootstock. Leaves sessile. Flowers tubular, lobed; lobes white outside, dark reddish brown within. Flowers opening at night, sweetly scented thus attracting insects.

Ht: up to 80 cm. **Fl**: Oct–Apr. **Distr**: T.

Mimulus gracilis

Slender, erect, perennial herb, slightly branched, smooth throughout. Leaves well-spaced, faintly toothed. Flowers 2-lipped, white, solitary, in axils of upper leaves; tube widening to throat.

Ht: up to 50 cm. **Fl**: Oct–Jan. **Distr**: T.

Limosella longiflora

Small, erect, aquatic herbs forming thick mats with stolons. Leaves linear, basal. Flowers solitary, long-stalked, white or lilac or blue.

Ht: up to 5 cm. **Fl**: Sep–May.
Distr: W, C, E, S.

Cycnium adonense

Mushroom Flower, Ink Plant; Inkblom

Small, semi-erect to erect, hemiparasitic herb, turning black when dried or bruised. Leaves sharply toothed. Flowers large, showy, pure white, trumpet-shaped, solitary or in pairs.

Ht: up to 30 cm. **Fl:** Sep–Jan. **Distr:** T.

Hebenstreitia comosa
Katstert

Slender, erect herb with smooth, slightly branched, leafy stems from woody rootstock. Leaves crowded, sessile, margins shortly toothed. Inflorescence an elongated spike, solitary or groups. Flowers tubular, 4-lobed, white with yellow or scarlet blotch near throat.

Ht: up to 1 m. **Fl:** Nov–Mar. **Distr:** T.

Selago densiflora
(= *Walafrida densiflora*)

Erect, closely leafy herb, much-branched from base. Leaves linear. Flowers small, tubular, white, in rounded heads at tips of branches; calyx 3-lobed.

Ht: up to 40 cm. **Fl:** Jan–May. **Distr:** T.

Selago muddii

Similar to *S. procera* (p. 174), but differs in having smaller, narrower leaves, white flowers and a more compact inflorescence.

Ht: up to 30 cm. **Fl**: Oct–Mar. **Distr**: E.

Selago tenuifolia
(= *Walafrida tenuifolia*)

Erect, closely leafy, woody shrublet, much-branched from base. Leaves linear. Flowers small, tubular, white, in rounded heads at tips of branches.

Ht: up to 40 cm. **Fl**: Sep–Mar. **Distr**: T.

BIGNONIACEAE
Catophractes alexandri
Swartdoring

Grey, erect, spiny shrub with axillary, paired spines. Leaves opposite, densely grey-velvety hairy. Flowers 1 or 2, axillary, sessile or terminal, crinkled, with green tubular and white spreading lobes, tinted pink. Fruit green with irregular bumps, callous-tipped.

Ht: up to 2 m. **Fl**: after good rains. **Distr**: N, W.

ACANTHACEAE

Thunbergia neglecta

Twiggy, branched, leafy shrublet with stems tending to twine, shortly hairy throughout. Leaves triangular, with 1 or 2 blunt projections on each side. Flowers solitary, axillary, tubular, white.

Ht: up to 40 cm. **Fl**: Oct–Dec. **Distr**: T.

Petalidium aromaticum var. *aromaticum*

Much-branched, erect, closely leafy shrublet, white-silky hairy throughout. Bracts large, brown, margins partly joined to enclose calyx. Flowers tubular, white with brown markings.

Ht: up to 1 m. **Fl**: Oct–May. **Distr**: N, E.

Chaetacanthus costatus

Small, erect, perennial herb with several stems from woody rootstock. Leaves opposite. Flowers bilabiate, white or pale white-mauve, axillary, solitary or few together; stamens 2; staminodes 2.

Ht: up to 20 cm. **Fl**: Sep–Jan. **Distr**: N, W, C.

Ruellia sp. aff. *R. patula*

Shrublet with twiggy stems from woody rootstock, thickly, grey-shaggy hairy throughout, sometimes spreading by means of stolons. Leaves opposite, ovate, often heart-shaped at base. Flowers tubular, long, narrow at base widening to funnel-shaped, white.

Ht: up to 30 cm. **Fl**: Nov–Feb. **Distr**: N, W, C, E.

Crabbea angustifolia

Prostrate, perennial herb with hairy, trailing stems from woody rootstock. Leaves erect, opposite, coarsely hairy, margins entire or wavy. Flowers white or yellow, in dense compound, axillary heads, surrounded by spiny bracts.

Fl: Jan–Mar. **Distr**: T.

Hypoestes forskaolii

Erect or spreading, many-stemmed, stoloniferous herb. Leaves broad, ovate, entire. Bracts glandular-hairy. Flowers tubular, lipped, white, pink or pale lilac with dark purple honey guides, in terminal or axillary inflorescences.

Ht: up to 80 cm. **Fl**: Feb–May. **Distr**: T.

Hypoestes triflora

Slender, laxly branched, perennial herb, spreading by stolons. Leaves ovate, margins slightly wavy. Bracts leaf-like. Flowers tubular, white, pink or pale lilac with dark purple honey guides.

Ht: up to 40 cm. **Fl**: Sep–Apr.
Distr; N, E.

Justicia anagalloides

Tufted, sometimes decumbent, perennial herb, slightly thinly bristly hairy throughout. Leaf pairs well-spaced, shortly stalked, ovate, tapering to base. Flowers 1–4, at end of unbranched, axillary stalk, white.

Ht: up to 20 cm. **Fl**: Oct–Feb.
Distr: T.

Justicia betonica

Low herb with slender, zigzag stems, much-branched from woody rootstock. Leaf pairs well spaced. Inflorescence terminal, elongated. Bracts ovate, veined, pointed, overlapping. Flowers white, slightly hairy.

Ht: up to 50 cm. **Fl**: Nov–Apr.
Distr: N, W, C, E.

PLANTAGINACEAE

Plantago lanceolata

Narrow-leaved Ribwort, Plantain; Kleintongblaar, Smalweëblaar

Small, erect, perennial herb. Leaves ± 4, in basal rosette. Inflorescence a short, thick, dense spike. Flowers small, cream-coloured.

Ht: up to 30 cm. **Fl**: Sep–Feb. **Distr**: T.

RUBIACEAE

Kohautia amatymbica

Small, slender, erect, perennial herb. Leaves few, opposite. Flowers tubular, cream-coloured above, greenish below, in terminal, few-flowered clusters, sweetly scented, opening in the afternoon.

Ht: up to 50 cm. **Fl**: Oct–Jan. **Distr**: T.

Kohautia cynanchica

Aandblom(metjie)

Slender, erect herb with several thinly hairy stems, leafy near base. Flowers solitary on slender stalks, in loose terminal inflorescences, tubular, cream-coloured.

Ht: up to 40 cm. **Fl**: Oct–Apr. **Distr**: T.

Otiophora cupheoides

Small, erect shrublet, closely leafy, much-branched, forming rounded bushes with thick woody rootstock. Leaves small, opposite. Flowers tubular, white, terminal.

Ht: up to 30 cm. **Fl**: Nov–Feb. **Distr**: N, W, E.

DIPSACACEAE

Cephalaria zeyheriana
Mock Scabious

Erect, perennial herb with slender, hairy stem. Leaves mostly basal, sessile or subsessile, deeply divided to main vein. Inflorescence a long-stalked, terminal flowerhead. Flowers white.

Ht: up to 60 cm. **Fl**: Dec–Feb. **Distr**: T.

Scabiosa columbaria
Wild Scabious, Morning Bride, Rice Flower; Bitterbos

Slender, erect, hairy, perennial herb, arising from woody rootstock. Basal leaves usually sessile, narrowly ovate, toothed. Stem leaves varying from deeply to 2-lobed. Flowers white to pink, in terminal, long-stalked flowerhead; calyx bristled.

Ht: up to 1 m. **Fl**: Oct–Jan. **Distr**: T.

CUCURBITACEAE

Momordica balsamina

African Cucumber, Balsam Apple, Balsamina

Perennial, herbaceous climber with many stems from tuberous rootstock. Leaves 5-lobed almost to middle. Tendrils simple, hairy or smooth. Flowers unisexual, solitary; male and female flowers white, green-veined. Fruit globose to ovoid, bright orange to red, sparsely tubercled.

Fl: Jul–Apr. **Distr**: T.

CAMPANULACEAE

Wahlenbergia virgata

Erect, perennial herb with few smooth or slightly hairy stems from woody rhizome. Leaves few, sparsely toothed. Flowers solitary, long-stalked, white or bluish.

Ht: up to 50 cm. **Fl**: Sep–Nov. **Distr**: N, E, S.

LOBELIACEAE

Cyphia stenopetala

Slender, perennial herb with twining stems from a tuber. Leaves subsessile, narrowly lanceolate, mostly basal. Flowers 2-lipped, white, pale pink or lilac.

Ht: up to 30 cm. **Fl**: Oct–Apr. **Distr**: T.

Lobelia angolensis

Slender, prostrate herb, producing runners which become matted together. Leaves small, ovate, light green, in whorls. Flowers small, white, terminal on lateral branches.

Fl: Aug–Dec. **Distr**: W, C, E, S.

ASTERACEAE

Vernonia colorata
subsp. *colorata*

Tall, many-stemmed shrub, sometimes a small tree. Florets white or pale mauve, in many large flowerheads.

Ht: up to 1.5 m. **Fl**: Apr–Aug. **Distr**: N, E.

Vernonia wollastonii

Tall, spreading shrub, thinly hairy throughout. Florets white or pale mauve, in terminal flowerheads, repeatedly forking.

Ht: up to 60 cm. **Fl**: Sep–Nov, sometimes later. **Distr**: N, E.

Stomatanthes africanus

Erect, thinly hairy, branched herb. Leaves narrowing to a point, sharply toothed. Florets white, in dense flowerheads, in flat-topped inflorescence; bracts pointed.

Ht: up to 40 cm. **Fl**: Oct–Feb. **Distr**: N, E.

Aster bakerianus

Herbaceous perennial with 1 or several erect or slightly decumbent, annual stems from perennial rootstock. Leaves variable, ovate-oblong, shortly hairy, toothed. Involucral bracts in 3 series, tinged purple. Ray-florets blue, mauve, rarely white; disc-florets yellow.

Ht: up to 45 cm. **Fl**: Sep–Dec. **Distr**: E, S.

Aster lydenburgensis

Slender, erect herb, slightly branched. Florets white to pale pink, in solitary, terminal capitula.

Ht: 60–80 cm. **Fl**: Sep–Feb, sometimes later. **Distr**: E.

Felicia clavipilosa
subsp. *transvaalensis*

Small, erect, many-stemmed, closely leafy, bushy herb, greyish woolly throughout. Florets white, blue or mauve, in compact flowerheads at tips of branchlets.

Ht: up to 30 cm. **Fl**: Oct–Feb, sometimes later. **Distr**: N, E.

Felicia muricata
subsp. *muricata*

Wild Aster; Bloublommetjie, Taaibloublommetjie

Shrubby, much-branched herb, shortly rough-hairy throughout. Leaves many, blunt. Flowerheads at tips of branches, solitary. Ray-florets mauve or white; disc-florets yellow.

Ht: 15–30 cm. **Fl**: Nov–Apr. **Distr**: T.

Pseudognaphalium oligandrum

Annual herb with stiffly erect, simple or branched stems from base, closely leafy, white-woolly. Leaves lanceolate. Heads bell-shaped, several together in tight clusters. Involucral bracts in 4 series, white.

Ht: up to 1 m. **Fl**: Dec–May. **Distr**: T.

Helichrysum argyrolepis

Soft-wooded subshrub with branched, grey-white felted, closely leafy stems from woody rootstock. Leaves linear, grey-white woolly above, felted below. Involucral bracts glossy white, in solitary flowerheads at ends of branches.

Ht: up to 30 cm. **Fl**: Nov–Apr. **Distr**: N, E, S.

Helichrysum argyrosphaerum
Wild Everlasting; Poprosie

Slender, annual herb with prostrate or decumbent, much-branched stems, closely leafy, woolly throughout. Involucral bracts papery, pink-white, in solitary capitula at ends of branches.

Ht: up to 10 cm. **Fl**: Jun–Dec. **Distr**: T.

Helichrysum caespititium
Speelwonderboom

Small, compact dwarf shrublet, closely leafy, mat-forming. Leaves small, silvery woolly. Flowerheads sessile, solitary or in small groups. Inner florets yellow, surrounded by white or pink involucral bracts.

Fl: Aug–Nov. **Distr**: T.

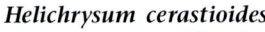

Helichrysum cerastioides var. *cerastioides*
Wolbossie, Sewejaartjie

Bushy herb with simple or branched, erect, decumbent or prostrate, closely leafy branches. Leaves linear, grey-woolly. Flowers many, yellow, surrounded by white, papery involucral bracts, in terminal, solitary or few flowerheads.

Ht: up to 20 cm. **Fl**: Jun–Oct. **Distr**: C, W, S, E.

Helichrysum lepidissimum

Dense, much-branched shrublet, closely leafy, grey-white-woolly. Leaves decreasing in size upwards, woolly-felted below. Flowers yellow, surrounded by white, creamy or pale straw-coloured involucral bracts, in many, branched, terminal flowerheads.

Ht: up to 50 cm. **Fl**: Apr–Aug. **Distr**: N, E, S, C.

Helichrysum platypterum

Robust, erect, perennial herb with simple stems, solitary or few together, thinly white-downy. Leaves sessile. Inflorescence terminal, in loose clusters of spherical heads. Involucral bracts silvery white.

Ht: up to 1 m. **Fl**: Feb–Apr. **Distr**: N, E.

Callilepis laureola
Ox-eye Daisy; Wildemargriet

Erect, perennial herb with stout, woody rootstock, smooth or with few silky hairs. Leaves stem-clasping. Flowerheads long-stalked, solitary or rarely few. Ray-florets white.

Ht: up to 75 cm. **Fl**: Oct–Feb. **Distr**: C, E, S.

Eclipta prostrata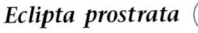
Eclipta

Prostrate or erect, annual herb with slender, white-hairy stems. Leaves opposite, toothed, roughly hairy. Ray-florets white, in terminal, globose capitula.

Ht: up to 60 cm. **Fl**: Jul–Feb, sometimes later. **Distr**: N, C, E, S.

Cosmos bipinnatus
Cosmos; Kosmos

Erect, branched, annual herb. Leaves opposite, deeply divided; lobes linear. Flowerheads large, terminal, solitary. Ray-florets white, pink, mauve or red.

Ht: up to 1.5 m. **Fl**: Dec–Apr. **Distr**: T.

Leucanthemum vulgare
(= *Chrysanthemum leucanthemum*)

Marguerite, Ox-eye Daisy, Dog Daisy, Moon Daisy; Margriet

Perennial herb with branched rootstock. Basal leaves long-stalked, smooth or sparsely hairy; stem leaves sessile. Flowering-stem simple or branched, with solitary, terminal flowerheads. Ray-florets white; disc-florets yellow.

Ht: up to 60 cm. **Fl**: Nov–Feb. **Distr**: E, S.

Senecio pentactinus

Robust, erect, closely leafy, many-stemmed, semiwoody subshrub. Leaves dark green above, paler below, conspicuously veined, sharply toothed. Flowers white in terminal, much-branched flowerheads.

Ht: up to 1.5 m. **Fl**: Nov–Feb. **Distr**: T.

Kleinia longiflora
Sambokbossie

Much-branched, succulent perennial. Leaves absent, rudimentary or small, succulent. Flowerheads solitary, conical. Ray-florets absent, disc-florets dirty white to yellow, protruding far beyond the involucral bracts.

Ht: up to 60 cm. **Fl**: Aug–Oct.
Distr: N, W, C, E.

Gazania krebsiana subsp. *serrulata*
Common Gazania; Kleingousblommetjie, Witgousblommetjie

Small, erect, tufted, perennial herb. Leaves many, basal, narrow, white-felted below. Flowerheads solitary, terminal on elongated stalks. Ray-florets white (bright yellow in Mpumalanga).

Ht: up to 10 cm. **Fl**: Aug–Mar.
Distr: T.

Gerbera ambigua (= *G. kraussii*)

Stemless, perennial herb spreading by underground runners. Leaves hairy, in basal rosette. Flowerheads terminal, long-stalked. Ray-florets white above, pink below, sometimes yellow.

Fl: Jun–Jan. **Distr**: T.

Gerbera viridifolia subsp. *viridifolia*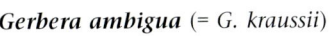
Griekwatee(bossie)

Small, erect, annual herb from thick rootstock, hairy throughout. Leaves basal. Florets white, yellow, pink or purple, in solitary, long-stalked, terminal capitula.

Ht: up to 20 cm. **Fl**: Sep–Nov.
Distr: T.

Pink Flowers

ARACEAE

Zantedeschia rehmannii
Red or Purple Arum; Persvarkblom

Erect annual with perennial rootstock. Leaves large, heart-shaped, long-stalked, dark green. Spathe folded from base to its length into a funnel, white to pink to maroon. Spadix finger-like, yellow.

Ht: up to 50 cm. **Fl**: Sep–Feb. **Distr**: E, S.

ASPHODELACEAE

Aloe greatheadii var. ***davyana***
(= *A. davyana*)

Robust plant, single or in groups of up to 10. Leaves many in a basal rosette, succulent, thick, fleshy, green with oblong blotches in transverse bands on upper surface, margins brown, armed with sharp teeth. Inflorescence branched, dense or lax raceme. Flowers tubular, pale pink to brick-red.

Ht: 15–30 cm, excluding inflorescence.
Fl: Jun–Jul. **Distr**: N, C.

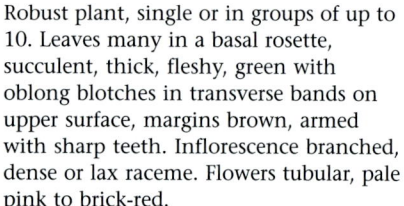

AMARYLLIDACEAE

Haemanthus humilis
subsp. ***hirsutus***
Velskoenblaar

Two basal leaves from globose bulb covered with brown tunic. Leaves broadly ovate or rotund, blunt, hairy, especially on margins. Inflorescence long-stalked, with terminal dense head of pale pink to white flowers surrounded by pink bracts; anthers yellow, exserted.

Ht: up to 20 cm. **Fl**: Nov–Mar.
Distr: E, S.

Boophone disticha

Cape Poison Bulb, Candelabra Flower, Sore-eye Flower; Gifbol, Kopseerblom

Perennial herb with large, partly underground bulb covered with tunic of many thin, brown, papery scales. Leaves basal, spreading fan-wise, produced after flowers. Inflorescence solitary, 70–100-flowered. Flowers deep pink or pale red.

Ht: up to 30 cm.
Fl: Sep–Nov: **Distr**: T.

Nerine platypetala

Plants solitary, with leaves and inflorescence stalk tall, slender from ovoid bulb. Leaves few, narrow, inrolled, smooth. Inflorescence a 7–15-flowered umbel. Flowers without tube, pink.

Ht: up to 40 cm. **Fl**: Jan–Feb. **Distr**: S, E.

Crinum bulbispermum

Orange River Lily; Rivierlelie

Erect, robust plant with large bulb. Leaves grey-green, sheathing at base to form false stems. Inflorescence a 6–16-flowered umbel. Flowers narrow, funnel-shaped, from deep pink to white with dull red stripes on keel.

Ht: up to 50 cm. **Fl**: Oct–Nov.
Distr: C, E, S, W.

Ammocharis coranica
Tumbleweed; Berglelie, Gifbol

Robust perennial with large, ovoid bulb with thick, shiny brown tunics. Leaves up to 15, spreading, basal. Inflorescence a 3–56-flowered umbel. Flowers tubular, pink or pinkish brown, sweetly scented.

Ht: up to 30 cm. **Fl**: Oct–Dec. **Distr**: T.

IRIDACEAE

Gladiolus crassifolius

Tall, erect plant growing solitary from globose corm covered with brown, matted fibres. Leaves 5–11, linear, forming a sheathing fan. Inflorescence a long, many-flowered spike. Flowers narrow, bell-shaped, pink, red, orange, mauve, purple or white.

Ht: up to 1 m. **Fl**: Feb–Apr. **Distr**: C, E, S.

Watsonia transvaalensis

Robust, erect herb with simple flowering-stem from globose corm covered with tunic of strong fibres. Leaves ± 4, basal, with thickened yellow margins. Flowers funnel-shaped, magenta-pink with deeper pink stripe down the middle.

Ht: up to 80 cm. **Fl**: Feb–Apr. **Distr**: N, E.

ORCHIDACEAE

Satyrium cristatum var. *cristatum*

Robust, erect, smooth, perennial herb. Basal leaves usually 2, overlapping one another. Flowers small, white to pale pink with purple to reddish brown lines and blotches along main vein of sepals and petals, which are fused for half their length with lip forming shallow sac below column.

Ht: up to 50 cm. **Fl**: Jan–Mar. **Distr**: T.

Satyrium longicauda var. *longicauda*

Slender, erect herb with large, unbranched, tuberous rootstock. Leaves usually a pair on separate shoot. Flowers sweetly scented, white or pink, in dense terminal spike. Lip hooded, with flap at apex.

Ht: up to 50 cm. **Fl**: Oct–Mar. **Distr**: N, W, E, S.

Satyrium neglectum subsp. *neglectum*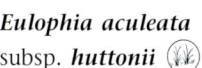

Robust, erect herb. Leaves absent to fully grown at flowering time. Flowers small to medium-sized, pink to dark red or orange to orange-yellow, usually sweetly scented, in terminal spike; lip small.

Ht: up to 1 m. **Fl**: Jan–Mar. **Distr**: E.

Disperis tysonii

Slender, erect plant. Leaves 3–6, cauline, alternate, sessile, lance-shaped. Flowers 2–14, pink to deep rose. Dorsal sepal conical-hooded, tipped backwards.

Ht: up to 20 cm **Fl**: Jan–Feb. **Distr**: E, S.

Eulophia aculeata subsp. *huttonii*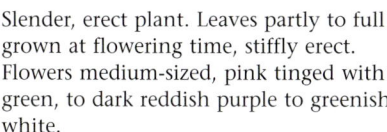

Slender, erect plant. Leaves partly to full grown at flowering time, stiffly erect. Flowers medium-sized, pink tinged with green, to dark reddish purple to greenish white.

Ht: up to 60 cm. **Fl**: Nov–Jan. **Distr**: E.

POLYGONACEAE

Persicaria attenuata subsp. *africana*

Robust, erect herb, softly hairy throughout. Ocrea fringed with hard, brown bristles. Flowers small, pink, in dense terminal, spike-like raceme.

Ht: up to 1.5 m. **Fl:** Nov–Mar. **Distr:** T.

Persicaria lapathifolia

Spotted Knotweed; Viltige-duisendknoop

Robust, erect, much-branched, perennial herb with few bristles on the reddish stems and petioles. Ocrea not fringed, tearing easily. Flowers small, deep pink, in dense terminal raceme.

Ht: up to 1 m. **Fl:** Oct–Mar. **Distr:** T.

Persicaria limbata

Stout, erect, perennial herb. Ocrea with conspicuous green, leaf-like limb, fringed with cilia. Flowers small, pink, in dense terminal raceme.

Ht: up to 50 cm. **Fl:** Sep–May. **Distr:** T.

Persicaria serrulata

Erect or semi-erect herb. Ocrea fringed with long cilia. Leaves long, tapering to both ends. Flowers small, deep pink, in lax terminal raceme.

Ht: up to 50 cm. **Fl:** Oct–May. **Distr:** T.

AMARANTHACEAE

Hermbstaedtia linearis

Woolflower; Katstertjie

Robust, erect herb with much-branched stems in upper half from woody rootstock. Leaves subsessile, linear. Inflorescence a dense, ± globose or shortly cylindrical spike. Flowers papery, pink or white; style long, exserted in lower flowers.

Ht: up to 50 cm. **Fl:** Sep–Apr. **Distr:** N, E.

Kyphocarpa angustifolia

Silky Burweed

Slender, erect herb, much-branched from woody base. Leaves opposite, linear. Flowers pungent, pink with white tips or straw-coloured, densely silky hairy, in terminal elongated inflorescences.

Ht: up to 60 cm. **Fl:** Dec–May. **Distr:** T.

Achyranthes aspera var. *aspera*

Burweed, Chaff Flower; Grootklits, Kafblom

Robust, erect, subwoody, perennial herb or shrublet, shortly hairy. Leaves opposite, elliptic, dark green above, paler below, hairy. Flowers small, pungent, straw-coloured to pinkish, terminal spikes.

Ht: up to 1.2 m. **Fl:** Sep–Mar. **Distr:** T.

PHYTOLACCACEAE

Phytolacca octandra

Forest Inkberry, Inkberry; Bobbejaandruif, Inkbessie

Erect shrublet with stout, reddish, branched stems from thick, swollen root. Leaves ovate, long-stalked. Flowers small, inconspicuous, green, in dense cylindrical head. Fruit globose, fleshy, blue-black.

Ht: up to 60 cm. **Fl:** Oct–Dec. **Distr:** T.

MESEMBRYANTHEMACEAE

Delospermum herbeum
Highveld White Vygie; Witbergvygie

Small, sprawling, succulent, perennial herb. Leaves fleshy, blue-green, triangular, deeply grooved. Flowers pale pink to white, axillary, many-petalled.

Ht: up to 20 cm. **Fl:** Sep–Mar. **Distr:** T.

Delosperma sutherlandii

Small, erect, succulent herb with usually single densely hairy stem from carrot-shaped, tuberous rootstock. Leaves fleshy, lanceolate, stem-clasping. Flowers pink, with many petals.

Ht: up to 30 cm. **Fl:** Nov–Jan. **Distr:** E, S.

PORTULACACEAE

Portulacaria afra
Porkbush; Spekboom

Fleshy, stout shrub or small tree. Leaves small, opposite, succulent, almost circular, pale greyish green, with each pair at right angles to the next along reddish stems. Flowers small, star-shaped, pale pink to purplish, in dense, terminal and axillary sprays.

Ht: up to 6 m. **Fl:** Oct–Nov. **Distr:** N, E.

CARYOPHYLLACEAE

Silene burchellii
var. ***burchellii***
Gunpowder Plant; Kruitbossie

Slender, erect, perennial herb from woody rootstock. Leaves mostly in a basal rosette, diminishing in size upwards. Flowers terminal, greenish white to deep pink, many in spike.

Ht: up to 40 cm. **Fl:** Nov–Mar. **Distr:** T.

Dianthus basuticus subsp. ***basuticus*** var. ***basuticus***

Slender, erect, perennial herb from woody rootstock. Leaves simple, linear-lanceolate, opposite, fused together basally, margins entire. Flowers solitary, terminal; petal margin entire, white to deep pink; stamens exserted.

Ht: up to 40 cm. **Fl**: Nov–Jan. **Distr**: E, S.

Dianthus mooiensis subsp. ***mooiensis*** var. ***mooiensis***

Perennial herb with woody base. Leaves opposite, mostly basal, narrow, tapering to a point. Flowers terminal, solitary, red, pink or white, rarely yellow; petals fringed.

Ht: up to 30 cm. **Fl**: Oct–Jan. **Distr**: T.

BRASSICACEAE

Heliophila carnosa

Erect, glabrous shrublet with annual flowering shoot from woody rootstock. Leaves crowded at base, filiform, entire or lobed in upper half, often fleshy. Flowers pink, mauve or white.

Ht: up to 60 cm. **Fl**: Sep–Jan. **Distr**: S.

CAPPARACEAE

Cleome hirta

Erect, somewhat woody herb with little-branched, glandular-hairy stems. Leaves aromatic, 5–9-foliolate, glandular-hairy. Flowers pink to purple, paler to base with yellow zone across middle. Fruit a narrow, linear capsule.

Ht: up to 50 cm. **Fl**: throughout the year. **Distr**: W, C, E.

Cleome maculata

Slender, erect, branched, annual herb. Leaves compound, with 3–5 linear leaflets. Flowers pink to mauve with bright yellow band edged with dark purple. Fruit a narrow, linear capsule.

Ht: up to 30 cm. **Fl**: Dec–Apr.
Distr: W, C.

Cleome rubella
Pretty Lady; Mooinooientjie

Erect, annual herb with glandular-hairy stems. Leaves aromatic, compound, with 5–7 glandular-hairy leaflets. Flowers mauve-pink to rose, without yellow bands.

Ht: up to 40 cm. **Fl**: Nov–Apr.
Distr: W, C.

FABACEAE
Indigofera filipes

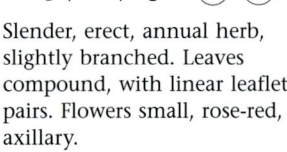

Slender, erect, annual herb, slightly branched. Leaves compound, with linear leaflet pairs. Flowers small, rose-red, axillary.

Ht: up to 50 cm. **Fl**: Dec–Apr.
Distr: T.

Indigofera heterotricha

Slender, erect herb with glandular-hairy stems from woody rootstock. Leaves compound, with 5 or 6 pairs of opposite leaflets. Flowers small, deep red, in axillary, long-stalked inflorescences.

Ht: up to 40 cm. **Fl**: Oct–Feb. **Distr**: T.

Indigofera hilaris

Perennial herb, closely leafy from stout, woody rootstock. Leaves compound, with usually 5 leaflets, ending in a short point. Flowers small, showy, bright pink, in dense, axillary clusters.

Ht: up to 40 cm. **Fl**: Aug–Nov. **Distr**: T.

Indigofera sordida

Robust, erect, perennial herb with much-branched stems densely covered with glandular hairs. Leaves compound, with up to 8 pairs of well-spaced opposite leaflets. Flowers pink, in axillary, long-stalked clusters.

Ht: up to 80 cm. **Fl**: Oct–Mar. **Distr**: N, W, C, E.

Indigastrum costatum subsp. *macrum*

Slender, erect, annual herb. Leaves compound, with 5–9 leaflets; terminal leaflets shorter than both petiole and rachis. Flowers small, pink, in axillary, long-stalked inflorescences.

Ht: up to 50 cm. **Fl**: Oct–Mar. **Distr**: N, W, C, E.

Tephrosia capensis

Herb with much-branched, procumbent stems from woody rootstock. Leaves compound, with 2–4 pairs of opposite leaflets and a terminal one; leaflets dark reddish brown-veined on undersurface. Flowers small, deep pink or purple.

Fl: Sep–Jan. **Distr**: T.

Lessertia stricta

Tall, erect herb with smooth, pale green stems. Leaves alternate, compound, with 4–8 pairs of opposite leaflets and a terminal one, hairy below, smooth above. Flowers white, pink, red, purple or blue, in long-stalked axillary clusters. Pod flat, yellow-green.

Ht: up to 1 m. **Fl**: Jan–Mar. **Distr**: N, C, E, S.

Pseudarthria hookeri var. ***hookeri***

Ferweelboontjie

Tall, robust, erect, much-branched perennial herb. Leaves 3-foliolate; leaflets densely hairy below. Inflorescence many-flowered, terminal, much-branched. Flowers small, various shades of pink.

Ht: up to 2 m. **Fl**: Jan–Feb. **Distr**: N, W, E.

Alysicarpus rugosus subsp. ***perennirufus***

Decumbent, spreading, perennial herb, much-branched from woody taproot. Leaves 1-foliolate. Calyx lobes with brown to orange cilia. Flowers pink, magenta or purple. Fruit moniliform, extending beyond persistent calyx.

Ht: 0.2–1 m. **Fl**: Nov–Mar. **Distr**: N, C, E, S.

Sphenostylis angustifolia

Shrublet with subwoody stems from thick, perennial rootstock. Leaves 3-foliolate. Flowers many, bright pink or violet, sweetly scented, axillary.

Ht: up to 50 cm. **Fl**: Oct–Nov. **Distr**: T.

GERANIACEAE

Monsonia angustifolia

Crane's Bill; Teebossie, Alsbos

Erect or semi-erect herb with reddish, hairy stems. Leaves alternate at base, opposite towards tips of stems, margins red-tinged, scalloped. Stipules spinescent. Inflorescence 1–3-flowered. Flowers white, mauve, pink, blue or sometimes yellow with dark venation.

Ht: up to 40 cm. **Fl**: Nov–Mar, sometimes later. **Distr**: T.

Monsonia attenuata

Erect, closely leafy, little-branched herb with reddish, hairy stems from tuberous rootstock. Leaves narrowly lanceolate, margin finely toothed. Flowers 1–3, terminal, deep pink or sometimes white.

Ht: up to 30 cm. **Fl**: Nov–Mar. **Distr**: T.

Monsonia burkeana
Dysentery Weed; Alsbossie, Angelbossie

Erect or semi-erect shrublet with numerous herbaceous or woody stems from rootstock. Leaves long-stalked, ovate, hairy, margins serrate. Flowers 1–4, large, showy, white, pink, mauve or rarely yellow, terminal.

Ht: up to 30 cm. **Fl**: Jan–Apr. **Distr**: N, W, C, S.

Erodium cicutarium

Alfileria, Common Storkbill; Muskuskruid, Oorlosie

Erect to procumbent, annual herb. Leaves in a basal rosette, flat on ground, deeply divided and again divided, toothed; upper leaves few. Flowers small, mauve-pink, in axillary, terminal umbels.

Fl: Jan. **Distr**: S, E, W.

Pelargonium luridum

Robust herb with stems from woody tuber. Leaves large, variable in shape, from shallowly to deeply lobed; lobes again divided. Inflorescence long-stalked, with 5–60 relatively large flowers arranged in pseudo-umbels. Flowers white, pink or yellowish to yellow-green.

Ht: up to 60 cm. **Fl**: Sep–Apr. **Distr**: T.

OXALIDACEAE

Oxalis obliquifolia

Small, erect herb with leaves and flowering-stem from small, ovoid bulb. Leaves many, 3-foliolate; leaflets with few marginal hairs. Flowers solitary, on stalk longer than leaves, bright pink with yellow centre.

Ht: up to 15 cm.
Fl: Nov–Mar. **Distr**: T.

EUPHORBIACEAE

Jatropha lagarinthoides

Slender, erect herb with annual stems from large, perennial, tuberous rootstock. Leaves alternate, finely toothed towards base. Flowers pink, yellow or cream-coloured, star-shaped, in terminal clusters. Fruit an ovoid 3-loculed berry.

Ht: up to 30 cm. **Fl**: Sep–Nov. **Distr**: C.

BALSAMINACEAE

Impatiens hochstetteri subsp. *hochstetteri*

Erect to procumbent, annual or perennial herb with stems often rooting at lower nodes. Leaves spirally arranged, sparsely hairy, toothed, with hairs between lobes. Flowers axillary, solitary or 2 or 3, whitish, pale pink or pale mauve, often with white or pale yellow dot at base.

Ht: up to 75 cm. **Fl**: Dec–Mar.
Distr: N, E, S.

Impatiens sylvicola

Low, scrambling or erect, annual or perennial herb with reddish tinged, hairy stems, branched, often rooting at lower nodes. Leaves spirally arranged, sparsely hairy, toothed. Flowers solitary or sometimes 2 or 3, pink, purplish pink or mauve with a deep mauve or reddish blotch at base.

Ht: up to 75 cm. **Fl**: Dec–Mar. **Distr**: N, E.

MALVACEAE

Pavonia columella

Erect to spreading, leafy shrub, sometimes sticky. Leaves 3–5-lobed, with middle lobe longer, heart-shaped at base, toothed. Flowers white, pale pink or pale mauve, solitary in upper axils.

Ht: 1–2 m. **Fl**: Feb–May. **Distr**: T.

Hibiscus pedunculatus

Slender, erect, much-branched, perennial shrublet, woody at base. Leaves simple or 3–5-lobed, stellate-hairy, margins toothed. Flowers large, bright pink, axillary.

Ht: up to 1 m. **Fl**: Nov–May. **Distr**: N, E.

STERCULIACEAE

Hermannia boraginiflora
Gombossie

Erect, much-branched shrublet with gland-tipped, star-like hairs. Leaves toothed in upper portion. Flowers pink or off-white with deep pink patches on lower half of inner face, solitary, axillary.

Ht: up to 60 cm. **Fl**: throughout the year. **Distr**: N, W, E.

Hermannia quartiniana subsp. *quartiniana*

Prostrate creeper or scrambler, with velvety, stellate-hairy, much-branched stems from woody rootstock. Leaves ovate, toothed. Flowers long-stalked, axillary, pink.

Fl: Nov–Jun. **Distr**: N, W, C, E.

ONAGRACEAE

Epilobium hirsutum

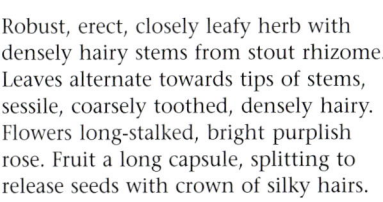

Robust, erect, closely leafy herb with densely hairy stems from stout rhizome. Leaves alternate towards tips of stems, sessile, coarsely toothed, densely hairy. Flowers long-stalked, bright purplish rose. Fruit a long capsule, splitting to release seeds with crown of silky hairs.

Ht: up to 2.5 m. **Fl**: Mar–May. **Distr**: W, C, E, S.

Oenothera rosea
Rose Evening Primrose, Evening Primrose; Rooskleurige-nagblom, Aandblom

Erect to decumbent, much-branched, perennial herb, densely hairy throughout. Leaves alternate, ovate, shallowly toothed, sometimes wavy, hairy on both surfaces. Flowers solitary, axillary, pink to magenta. Fruit a club-shaped capsule, with narrow winged angles.

Ht: up to 50 cm. **Fl**: Oct–Jan. **Distr**: T.

ERICACEAE

Erica woodii

Much-branched, woody shrublet with crowded, linear leaves. Flowers small, globose, dull pink or purple, many along lateral branches; styles protruding.

Ht: up to 40 cm. **Fl**: Feb–Apr. **Distr**: N, E.

GENTIANACEAE

Chironia palustris
subsp. ***transvaalensis***

Bitterwortel

Slender, erect, annual herb forming clumps, branched towards top of plant. Leaves broad at base, tapering to long tip. Flowers terminal, rose-pink; anthers slightly twisted.

Ht: up to 70 cm. **Fl**: Dec–Jan. **Distr**: T.

Chironia purpurascens
subsp. ***humilis***

Slender, erect, biennial or perennial herb with 4-angled stems from taproot. Leaves mostly in basal pairs. Flowers deep magenta-pink; anthers strongly twisted.

Ht: up to 50 cm. **Fl**: Oct–Feb. **Distr**: T.

APOCYNACEAE

Subfamily Apocynoideae

Adenium multiflorum

Impala Lily, Sabie Star; Impalalelie

Succulent shrub with swollen stems often tuberous at base. Leaves clustered at ends of branches. Flowers large, showy, white or pink, with pink to dark red crisped margin.

Ht: 0.6–3 m. **Fl**: May–Aug. **Distr**: N, E.

Subfamily Asclepiadoideae
Asclepias adscendens

Prostrate to erect herb with thinly hairy stems, branched from base, from perennial, woody rootstock. Leaves shortly stalked, triangular, broadest at base. Flowers dull pink or mauve, with spreading lobes, in terminal umbel.

Ht: up to 30 cm. **Fl**: Sep–Feb. **Distr**: C, E, S, W.

CONVOLVULACEAE

Ipomoea gracilisepala

Annual with several prostrate, shortly hairy stems from base. Leaves erect, upper surface dark green, smooth, paler, densely hairy below. Flowers small, funnel-shaped, pink or mauve with darker centre, rarely white.

Fl: Dec–Mar. **Distr**: N, W, C.

Ipomoea magnusiana

Perennial, climbing or prostrate herb. Stems annual, few to many, densely hairy. Leaves digitately 3–5-lobed, divided almost to base, yellow-green above, grey-white-hairy below. Flowers funnel-shaped, long-stalked, axillary, white outside, deep pink or magenta inside, with white zone below stamens.

Fl: Dec–May. **Distr**: N, W, C, E.

LAMIACEAE

Hemizygia modesta

Many-stemmed herb with annual stems from perennial, woody rootstock. Leaves subsessile, slightly to very rough-hairy. Inflorescence simple, in 2-flowered rows. Flowers tubular, white, pink to pale mauve; stamens exserted.

Ht: up to 25 cm. **Fl**: Sep–Dec. **Distr**: E.

Hemizygia transvaalensis

Tall, soft shrublet with hairy, annual stems from perennial, woody rootstock. Leaves subsessile, hairy on both surfaces. Inflorescence lax, paniculate, in well-spaced rows of 3–6 flowers. Bracts ovate, pinkish purple. Flowers tubular, white to mauve or lilac-pink.

Ht: up to 1 m. **Fl**: Jun–Dec, sometimes indefinite. **Distr**: E.

SCROPHULARIACEAE
Nemesia fruticans

Slender, erect, much-branched, annual herb. Flowers few, in clusters at ends of branches, pink, blue, lavender or white with a yellow crest, 2-lipped, the tube fused into a spur.

Ht: up to 60 cm. **Fl**: throughout the year. **Distr**: T.

Craterostigma wilmsii
Moles' Spectacles

Small, erect herb from woody rootstock. Leaves in basal rosette. Flowers tubular, 2-lipped; lower lip bright rose (common name refers to two filaments which are attached to the yellow blotch on lower lip and curve around the upper corolla lobe).

Ht: up to 30 cm. **Fl**: Oct–Feb. **Distr**: T.

Graderia subintegra
Wild Penstemon, Ground Bulb

Erect or semi-erect, perennial herb with reddish shortly hairy stems. Leaves sharply toothed. Flowers funnel-shaped, pink to purple, lobed; lobes unequal, with swelling on one side.

Ht: up to 20 cm. **Fl**: Aug–Mar. **Distr**: W, C, E, S.

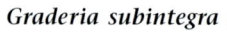

Sopubia cana var. *cana*

Small, erect, much-branched, grey-hairy, perennial herb from woody rootstock. Flowers small, pink, in terminal, many-flowered panicles.

Ht: up to 30 cm. **Fl**: Dec–Mar. **Distr**: T.

Cycnium racemosum

Slender, erect, usually unbranched, perennial herb, turning black when dried. Leaves sharply toothed. Flowers large, trumpet-shaped, white or pink, solitary or in terminal pairs.

Ht: up to 50 cm. **Fl**: Dec–Mar. **Distr**: N, E.

Cycnium tubulosum

Slender, erect, perennial herb from rhizomatous rootstock. Leaves simple, opposite, narrow. Flowers solitary, tubular, mauve-pink, blue or white with yellow throat, in axils of upper leaves.

Ht: up to 60 cm. **Fl**: Oct–Apr. **Distr**: T.

Striga forbesii

Giant Mealie Witchweed, Witchweed; Rooiblom

Robust, erect herb, coarsely hairy throughout, drying black. Leaves opposite, toothed. Flowers tubular, pink to scarlet, in axillary clusters.

Ht: up to 30 cm. **Fl**: Jan–May. **Distr**: T.

PEDALIACEAE

Sesamum alatum

Tall, slender, erect, little-branched, smooth herb. Basal leaves irregularly lobed; upper leaves simple, narrow, faintly toothed. Flowers solitary, axillary, funnel-shaped, 2-lipped, rose-pink. Fruit a capsule, tapering to a terminal beak, splitting open when ripe.

Ht: up to 1 m. **Fl**: Jan–Mar. **Distr**: N, W, C, E.

Dicerocaryum senecioides

Boot-Protector, Devil's Thorn, Wild Foxglove; Beesdubbeltjie, Dubbeltjie, Duiweltjies

Perennial herb with long, trailing, smooth stems with deep taproot. Leaves opposite, deeply irregularly lobed and toothed. Flowers solitary, axillary, funnel-shaped, deep pink with deep pink veining in throat. Fruit a hard, ovoid disc with 2 erect straight spines near centre on upper side.

Fl: Feb–May. **Distr**: T.

GESNERIACEAE

Streptocarpus dunnii

Stemless perennial herb. Leaf solitary, leathery, usually withering away at one end, grey-hairy on both surfaces, margins scalloped, often wavy. Inflorescences borne in succession on leaf-bases, flowers clustered. Flowers tubular, rose-pink or dull red, hairy with short gland-tipped hairs.

Fl: Nov–Mar. **Distr**: E, S.

ASTERACEAE

Campuloclinium macrocephalum
(= *Eupatorium macrocephalum*)

Pom-pom Weed; Pompombossie

Robust, erect, branched herb, roughly hairy throughout. Flowerheads terminal, globose, in flat-topped inflorescence. Florets pink-mauve.

Ht: up to 1 m. **Fl**: Jan–Mar. **Distr**: C.

Tenrhynea phylicifolia

Shrubby perennial with smooth, closely leafy branches. Leaves alternate, narrowly lance-shaped, grey-hairy below. Flowerheads in small, terminal clusters. Involucral bracts papery milky white to pink, in many rows.

Ht: up to 1 m. **Fl**: Feb–May. **Distr**: N, E.

Helichrysum rugulosum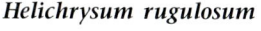

Slender, erect, perennial herb, closely leafy, much-branched from base. Leaves sessile, grey-woolly on undersurface. Florets pink fading to white, in terminal, globose, compact flowerheads.

Ht: up to 30 cm. **Fl**: Nov–Mar. **Distr**: E, C, S, W.

Helichrysum wilmsii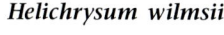

Subshrub with long, loose branches, glandular-hairy and white-woolly. Leaves scattered, tapering to fine point. Flowerheads showy, solitary, terminal. Involucral bracts papery white to pale pink.

Ht: up to 30 cm. **Fl**: Nov–May. **Distr**: N, E.

Yellow/Orange Flowers

XYRIDACEAE

Xyris gerrardii

Tufted perennial with hard, compact rhizome covered with dark, sheathing, shiny leaf-bases. Leaves grass-like, many, linear. Spike long-stalked, 5–8-flowered. Flowers yellow.

Ht: up to 30 cm. **Fl**: Nov–Jan. **Distr**: N, C, E.

COMMELINACEAE

Commelina africana var. ***africana***

Yellow Wandering Jew

Straggling, perennial herb from rootstock. Leaves with sheathing base. Flowers yellow, emerging from a folded spathe.

Ht: up to 50 cm. **Fl**: Oct–Mar. **Distr**: N, C, E, S.

COLCHICACEAE

Gloriosa superba

Flame Lily, Superb Lily; Geelboslelie, Rooiboslelie

Climber or semiclimber with slender stems from underground rootstock. Leaves ovate with a long tip curling up into a tendril. Flowers showy, bright scarlet or yellow; petals reflexed, crisped.

Fl: Nov–Mar. **Distr**: N, E.

Littonia modesta

Butter Lily, Yellow Lily; Geelklokkies

Herbaceous semiclimber, similar to *Gloriosa*. Leaves opposite, bright green, tips with long slender tendrils. Flowers axillary, single, long-stalked, pendulous, orange.

Fl: Nov–Jan. **Distr**: N, E, S.

Littonia rigidifolia

Similar to *L. modesta*, but differs in having rigid leaves and greenish yellow flowers.

Fl: Nov–Jan. **Distr**: N, W.

ASPHODELACEAE

Bulbine abyssinica

Robust geophyte with the flowering-stem from short rootstock with fleshy roots. Leaves linear-lanceolate, ending in a point, with white marginal wings at base, in a basal rosette. Flowers yellow, in dense terminal raceme.

Ht: up to 40 cm. **Fl**: Oct–Feb. **Distr**: T.

Bulbine narcissifolia
Geelslangkop, Slangkop

Similar to other members of *Bulbine* but differs in having broad, flat leaves.

Ht: up to 50 cm. **Fl**: Oct–Feb. **Distr**: W, C, S.

ASPHODELACEAE

Kniphofia linearifolia

Robust, erect perennial, usually in groups. Leaves 8–16, linear, erect, folding back with their weight at maturity, strongly keeled. Inflorescence a long-stalked, terminal, ovoid flowerhead. Flowers pendulous, pinkish red in bud, yellow to yellowish green at maturity.

Ht: up to 1.5 m. **Fl**: Jan–Mar. **Distr**: E, S.

Kniphofia porphyrantha
Red-hot Poker

Plants in groups, rarely solitary. Leaves 10–12, yellow-green, narrowly keeled below. Inflorescence a subglobose, long-stalked flowerhead. Flowers orange-flamed tipped with yellow, spreading in bud, becoming pendulous, lemon-yellow later.

Ht: up to 60 cm. Fl: Oct–Feb. Distr: C, S, E.

Kniphofia rigidifolia

Stout, erect perennial, growing in groups. Leaves 12–16, erect, yellow-green. Inflorescence a dense, terminal, ovoid flowerhead, not overtopping leaves. Flowers flame- to orange-red in bud, becoming yellow-green to greenish later.

Ht: up to 80 cm. **Fl**: Oct–Nov. **Distr**: E.

Aloe lutescens

Robust, erect, with short stems with offshoots forming dense clumps. Leaves up to 30 forming rosettes, dull green, turning yellow when sun-scorched, margins with pink-brownish teeth. Inflorescence 3-branched, up to 4 appearing together. Flowers tubular, red in bud, yellow open.

Ht: up to 1.2 m. **Fl**: Jun–Jul. **Distr**: N, E.

Aloe nubigena

Attractive, robust succulent, suckering, forming small clusters with roots wedged in crevices. Leaves in rosettes, bright green, margins entire, sometimes minutely toothed. Inflorescence 10–15-flowered, in capitula, racemose. Flowers tubular, orange with green tips.

Ht: up to 40 cm. **Fl**: Nov–Mar. **Distr**: E.

ERIOSPERMACEAE

Eriospermum flagelliforme

Geophyte with single underground tuber with tuft of bristles formed from old leaf remains at top. Single leaf appearing after inflorescence. Inflorescence much-branched. Flowers yellow, single at ends of branches.

Ht: up to 10 cm. **Fl**: Aug–Feb. **Distr**: T.

AMARYLLIDACEAE

Cyrtanthus breviflorus

Leaves 1–6, filiform, absent or present at flowering time. Flowers tubular, bell-shaped, in a 1–3-flowered umbel.

Ht: up to 30 cm. **Fl**: indefinite. **Distr**: E.

HYPOXIDACEAE

Hypoxis argentea var. *argentea*
Tulp

Slender, erect, herbaceous geophyte with large bulb with matted leaf remains at the top. Leaves many, grass-like, thinly hairy. Inflorescence axis short, slender. Flowers many, bright yellow, thinly hairy.

Ht: up to 15 cm. **Fl**: Nov–Apr. **Distr**: T.

Hypoxis iridifolia
(= *H. obtusa*)

Robust, herbaceous geophyte with large rootstock covered with leaf remains at the top, with roots spreading laterally. Leaves at flowering time, shiny, smooth or white-woolly along margins and midrib. Flowers yellow inside, green, white-hairy outside.

Ht: up to 40 cm. **Fl**: Aug–Jan, especially after fires. **Distr**: T.

Hypoxis rigidula var. *rigidula*

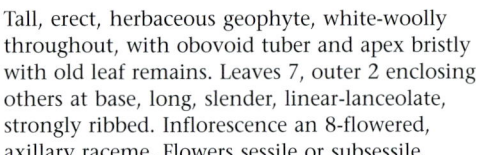

Tall, erect, herbaceous geophyte, white-woolly throughout, with obovoid tuber and apex bristly with old leaf remains. Leaves 7, outer 2 enclosing others at base, long, slender, linear-lanceolate, strongly ribbed. Inflorescence an 8-flowered, axillary raceme. Flowers sessile or subsessile, star-shaped, bright yellow.

Ht: up to 30 cm. **Fl**: Sep–Dec. **Distr**: T.

IRIDACEAE

Moraea moggii subsp. *moggii*

Tall, slender, erect plants growing solitarily from corm with pale tunics covered by matted fibres. Leaf solitary, linear. Spathe herbaceous. Flowers yellow with bright yellow nectar guides edged with purple.

Ht: up to 70 cm. **Fl**: Feb–Apr. **Distr**: E.

Crocosmia aurea var. *aurea*
Montbretia

Tall, erect, herbaceous perennial, from globose corm with membranous, papery, brown tunic. Leaves few to many in 2 ranks, stem-clasping, with distinct midribs. Inflorescences tall, branched, 5–10-flowered spikes. Flowers large, attractive, brilliant yellow-orange, in zigzag pattern. Popular garden subject.

Ht: up to 50 cm. **Fl**: Feb. **Distr**: N, E, S.

Tritonia nelsonii

Slender, erect, herbaceous perennial. Corm conical, covered with tunic of coarse, dark brown fibres. Leaves 4–8, erect, spreading fan-wise. Flowers funnel-shaped, orange to red, transparent, delicately veined, in few- to many-flowered spike; anthers black-violet.

Ht: 30–90 cm. **Fl**: Dec–Mar. **Distr**: T.

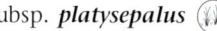

Gladiolus longicollis subsp. *platysepalus*

Erect plant growing solitarily from globose corm with dark brown, netted, fibrous tunic. Leaves reduced, distinctly ribbed. Flowers tubular, with short, acute lobes, yellow, white or cream-coloured, often flushed and veined purplish to brown or green, sweetly scented, in 1–3-flowered spike.

Ht: up to 80 cm. **Fl**: Oct–Dec. **Distr**: N, C, E, S.

ORCHIDACEAE

Ansellia africana
(= *A. gigantea*)

Tiger Orchid, Leopard Orchid, Tree Orchid

Robust plant forming thick clumps in tree branches. Pseudobulbous stems thick. Leaves alternate, thick, tough, stiff, parallel-veined. Flowers pale yellow or lightly marked with small, reddish brown spots.

Ht: up to 1 m. **Fl**: Jul–Nov. **Distr**: N, W, E.

Ansellia africana

Different form of the above, having pale or bright yellow flowers heavily dotted with small or large, reddish brown spots, hence the common name Leopard Orchid.

Eulophia angolensis

Robust, erect plant with flowering-stem from tuberous rootstock. Leaves basal, folded, stiffly erect. Flowers 4–10, terminal, bright lemon-yellow.

Ht: up to 1.4 m. **Fl**: Oct–Mar. **Distr**: N, W, C, E.

Eulophia leontoglossa

Stout, erect plant with short, curved flowering-stem at the top. Leaves stiffly erect. Flowers 7–35, densely massed, narrow, white to pale yellow or pink; midlobe with toothed edges and crests of yellow to yellow-brown, slender papillae.

Ht: up to 30 cm. **Fl**: Oct–Jan. **Distr**: N, C, E, S.

Eulophia ovalis subsp. *bainesii*

Robust, erect plant. Leaves fully developed at flowering time. Flowers up to 18, scentless, pale straw-yellow, brownish purple at base, with few dark speckles inside, with main veins yellow.

Ht: up to 60 cm. **Fl**: Dec–Jan. **Distr**: T.

Eulophia tuberculata

Slender, erect plant. Leaves absent at flowering time, spreading, fleshy, stiff. Flowers 10–30, small, yellow or dull white, tinged maroon with veins reddish purple, inside.

Ht: up to 40 cm. **Fl:** Sep–Nov. **Distr:** W.

Eulophia welwitschi

Slender, erect herb with perennial, underground rhizome. Leaves partly to full grown at flowering time. Flowers showy, yellow with cream-coloured lip and dark maroon side lobes, in dense, terminal clusters.

Ht: up to 90 cm. **Fl:** Nov–Jan. **Distr:** T.

MOLLUGINACEAE

Psammotropha myriantha

Small, erect, much-branched, perennial herb. Leaves linear in basal rosette. Flowers small, greenish yellow, in dense, terminal, well-spaced clusters.

Ht: up to 20 cm. **Fl:** Oct–Nov. **Distr:** T.

PORTULACACEAE

Talinum arnotii

Semi-erect, rarely decumbent shrublet with slightly hairy, succulent stems from long, branched tubers. Leaves narrowly ovate to broadly elliptic, with irregularly recurved margins. Inflorescence axillary, 1–3-flowered. Flowers yellow.

Ht: up to 40 cm. **Fl:** Nov–Apr. **Distr:** T.

Talinum caffrum

Similar to *T. arnotii*, but differs in having solitary flowers and linear to oblong leaves.

Fl: Nov–Mar. **Distr**: T.

RANUNCULACEAE

Ranunculus baurii

Perennial, hairless, branched herb. Leaves few, basal, circular, white-veined, long-stalked with stalk attached to centre of leaf, evenly toothed. Flowers yellow, slender-stalked.

Ht: up to 60 cm. **Fl**: Oct–Nov. **Distr**: E, S.

Ranunculus multifidus

Buttercup, Wild Buttercup; Botterblom, Kankerblare

Slender, erect, perennial herb. Leaves mostly basal, hairy, long-stalked, deeply divided, each further divided, deeply toothed. Flowers solitary, terminal, bright yellow, long-stalked; stamens many.

Ht: up to 75 cm. **Fl**: Sep–Apr, sometimes later. **Distr**: T.

PAPAVERACEAE

Argemone ochroleuca subsp. *ochroleuca*

White-flowered Mexican Poppy, Mexican Poppy; Witblom-bloudissel, Bloudissel

Robust, erect, annual herb with greyish stems, sparsely prickly, containing a yellowish juice. Leaves alternate, sessile, deeply divided, spiny. Flowers pale yellow or creamy white, solitary, terminal, sessile.

Ht: up to 90 cm. **Fl**: Aug–Mar. **Distr**: T.

Papaver aculeatum
Californian Poppy, Red Poppy, Thorny Poppy; Doringpapawer, Wildepapawer

Erect, annual herb with simple or branched stems, densely covered with yellowish patent spines. Leaves in a basal rosette, deeply lobed, densely hairy, with spines on midrib and dentations. Flowers saucer-shaped, salmon-pink or orange-red.

Ht: up to 90 cm. **Fl**: Nov–Jan.
Distr: T.

CAPPARACEAE

Cleome angustifolia
subsp. ***petersiana***
Peultjiesbos

Tall, erect herb, simple or branched. Leaves compound, with 3–9 linear-filiform leaflets. Flowers yellow with purple portion at base, in lax terminal raceme; stamens exserted, curled upwards at tips.

Ht: up to 80 cm. **Fl**: Dec–Mar.
Distr: N, E.

CRASSULACEAE

Kalanchoe paniculata

Robust, erect, perennial herb, with single stem from swollen rootstock. Leaves succulent, broadly ovate, in opposite pairs, folded lengthwise. Inflorescence a flat-topped thyrse. Flowers tubular, yellowish green to deep yellow.

Ht: up to 1.2 m. **Fl**: May–Sep.
Distr: C, S.

Kalanchoe thyrsiflora
White Lady; Geelplakkie

Robust, erect, unbranched, succulent herb, from swollen rootstock. Leaves sessile, opposite, grey-green tinged red, in large basal rosette, becoming smaller upwards. Inflorescence a dense, terminal, many-flowered elongated thyrse. Flowers tubular, yellow or greenish yellow, tipped with red.

Ht: up to 1.5 m. **Fl**: Feb–Jul. **Distr**: S, C.

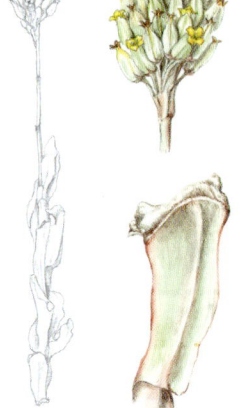

Crassula vaginata subsp. *vaginata*

Erect perennial from tuberous rootstock, with single rosette, with leaf pairs spirally arranged. Leaves lance-shaped, with stout marginal cilia. Inflorescence a flat-topped, terminal thyrse. Flowers tubular, yellow to white.

Ht: up to 50 cm. **Fl**: Jan–Apr. **Distr**: N, E, C.

VAHLIACEAE

Vahlia capensis subsp. *vulgaris* var. *linearis*

Small, erect, perennial herb with many closely leafy stems from woody rootstock. Leaves opposite, linear. Flowers axillary, paired, yellow; stamens exserted.

Ht: up to 20 cm. **Fl**: Nov–Feb. **Distr**: T.

ROSACEAE

Agrimonia procera

Agrimony; Akkermonie, Geelklits

Robust, erect, perennial herb with densely hairy stems from woody rootstock. Leaves alternate, divided; leaflets 4 or 5 pairs, elliptic, toothed. Flowers yellow, in terminal, dense, elongated raceme. Fruit an achene, crowned with hooked bristles.

Ht: up to 1.2 m. **Fl**: Jan–Apr. **Distr**: T.

FABACEAE

Elephantorrhiza elephantina

Eland's Bean, Eland's Wattle, Elephant's Root; Baswortel, Elandsboontjie, Elandswortel

Dwarf shrub with annual stems from woody rhizome. Leaves compound, with 2–4 pinnae pairs; leaflets 12–45 pairs, linear, asymmetric basally. Flowers small, yellowish white, in dense, axillary raceme.

Ht: up to 30 cm. **Fl**: Oct–Nov. **Distr**: T.

Chamaecrista mimosoides

Fish-bone Cassia

Slender, erect herb with thinly hairy, annual stems from perennial, woody rootstock. Leaves with many pairs of opposite leaflets. Flowers pale cream-coloured to yellow, axillary on long stalks.

Ht: up to 60 cm. **Fl**: Jan–Mar. **Distr**: T.

Senna italica subsp. ***arachoides***
Eland's Senna; Elandsertjie, Grondboontjie

Perennial herb with decumbent, trailing stems from woody rootstock. Leaves compound, with 3–6 pairs of shortly stalked, obovate leaflets. Flowers bright yellow, turning brown-veined with age. Pods flat, brown, with median line of crests.

Fl: Sep–Apr. **Distr**: T.

Lotononis eriantha

Small, erect herb with semi-erect to prostrate, hairy stems from woody rootstock. Stipules large, leaf-like. Leaves compound, with 3 ovate, hairy leaflets. Flowers few, yellow, in terminal, compact clusters.

Ht: 15–20 cm. **Fl**: Jan–Mar. **Distr**: N, C, E, S.

Lotononis listii
Geelklawer

Prostrate, perennial herb with smooth, spreading branches. Leaves 3-foliolate. Flowers yellow, in few- to many-flowered, axillary raceme. Pod flattened, semicircular, folded.

Fl: Sep–Mar. **Distr**: T.

Pearsonia cajanifolia subsp. ***cryptantha***

Erect shrublet with closely leafy, much-branched, densely hairy stems from woody rootstock. Leaves 3-foliolate; leaflets densely hairy. Flowers bright yellow, in terminal, 8–30-flowered clusters.

Ht: up to 1.5 m. **Fl**: Nov–Mar. **Distr**: T.

Pearsonia sessilifolia subsp. ***filifolia***

Small, erect herb, much-branched from perennial, woody rootstock. Leaflets 5–10 times as long as broad. Flowers small, yellow, turning orange with age.

Ht: up to 30 cm. **Fl**: Aug–Dec. **Distr**: E, S.

Pearsonia sessilifolia subsp. ***marginata***

Slender-stemmed, erect herb from woody rootstock. Leaflets hairy, less than 5 times as long as broad. Flowers small, yellow, at branch ends.

Ht: up to 80 cm. **Fl**: Nov–Apr. **Distr**: N, E.

Dichilus lebeckioides

Silver Bullet; Geellusern

Erect, much-branched, virgate shrublet. Leaves alternate, 3-foliolate, linear-oblong. Flowers yellow, up to 4 at ends of branchlets; calyx with lanceolate, acuminate teeth, nearly equalling wings.

Ht: up to 1 m. **Fl**: Nov–Mar. **Distr**: C, S, W, E.

Crotalaria brachycarpa

Slender, erect herb with many stems from woody rootstock, forming clumps. Leaves 3-foliolate. Flowers bright yellow, in terminal cluster; keel angular with narrow twisted beak.

Ht: up to 30 cm. **Fl**: Oct–Mar. **Distr**: C, S, W.

Crotalaria distans subsp. *distans*

Erect or semi-erect herb, shortly hairy. Leaves 3-foliolate; leaflets linear to elliptic, hairy below. Flowers yellow flushed with red or purplish; keel angular with long, narrow, twisted beak. Pod oblong-obovoid, 40-seeded.

Ht: up to 1.3 m. **Fl**: Dec–Apr. **Distr**: T.

Crotalaria laburnifolia subsp. *australis*

Erect, perennial herb, becoming woody, thinly hairy or smooth. Leaves 3-foliolate; leaflets narrow, elliptic; petiole long. Inflorescence a many-flowered raceme. Flowers large, showy.

Ht: up to 2 m. **Fl**: Jan–Mar. **Distr**: T.

Crotalaria lanceolata

Erect, annual herb with little-branched, hairy stems. Leaves 3-foliolate; leaflets narrowly lanceolate. Inflorescence a terminal, many-flowered raceme. Standard yellow, veined reddish purple. Keel shallowly rounded, with incurved beak.

Ht: up to 1.7 m. **Fl**: Nov–Mar. **Distr**: N, E.

Crotalaria sphaerocarpa

Mealie Crotalaria; Mielie-crotalaria

Erect, annual herb, much-branched from base. Leaves 3-foliolate; leaflets variable, linear to lanceolate. Flowers small, yellow; keel angled in beak. Pods small, oblong.

Ht: up to 1 m. **Fl**: Jan–Feb. **Distr**: T.

Argyrolobium tomentosum

Much-branched, slender-stemmed shrub. Leaves 3-foliolate; leaflets ovate, hairy on both surfaces. Flowers few, yellow fading to orange, axillary.

Ht: up to 1.5 m. **Fl**: throughout the year. **Distr**: N, E, S.

Lotus discolor subsp. *discolor*

Erect, perennial herb with many sparsely branched stems from woody rootstock. Leaves compound, with 1 terminal and 2 pairs of lateral leaflets, mottled. Flowers cream-coloured or pale yellow.

Ht: up to 50 cm. **Fl**: Oct–Dec. **Distr**: N, C, E, S.

Tephrosia elongata var. *elongata*

Robust, erect herb with several stems from woody rootstock. Leaves 1- or 2-jugate, lower occasionally simple; leaflets lanceolate, smooth or hairy. Flowers orange, in long-stalked, axillary inflorescences.

Ht: up to 60 cm. **Fl**: Oct–Mar. **Distr**: T.

Stylosanthes fruticosa

Wild Lucerne

Semi-erect to erect, perennial herb, much-branched from woody rootstock. Leaves 3-foliolate; leaflets conspicuously paler-veined, ending in a sharp point. Flowers yellow with red flush.

Ht: up to 45 cm. **Fl**: Sep–Mar. **Distr**: T.

Zornia capensis

Perennial herb with procumbent, smooth stems from woody rootstock. Leaves compound, with 4 leaflets; leaflets black-dotted. Flowers yellow, surrounded by shoe-like bracts. Pod with 4 or 5 segments, covered with large glands.

Fl: Oct–Mar. **Distr**: T.

Rhynchosia adenodes

Prostrate herb with thinly hairy, slender, trailing stems from woody rootstock. Leaves 3-foliolate; leaflets ovate, gland-dotted on undersurface. Flowers yellow, in axillary, long-stalked inflorescences.

Fl: Sep–Jan. **Distr**: W, C, E, S.

Rhynchosia monophylla

Perennial herb with trailing stems from woody rootstock. Leaves simple, occasionally compound, then with 3 leaflets, broadly ovate. Flowers few, small, yellow or orange with red veins, axillary.

Fl: Jul–Nov. **Distr**: T.

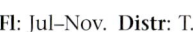

Rhynchosia nervosa var. *nervosa*

Robust, prostrate herb with long, trailing, hairy stems from woody rootstock. Leaves 3-foliolate; leaflets broadly ovate, hairy, prominently veined below. Flowers yellow, in well-spaced, axillary inflorescences.

Fl: throughout summer. **Distr**: T.

Rhynchosia nitens

Ferweelboontjie

Small, much-branched, woody shrub, silvery hairy throughout. Leaves 3-foliolate; leaflets ovate, shiny, dark green above, paler, velvety hairy below. Flowers bright yellow, with reflexed standard and purple mark at tip of keel.

Ht: up to 1.2 m. **Fl**: Sep–May. **Distr**: T.

Eriosema nutans

Perennial herb or subshrub with erect or decumbent, branched, hairy stems from woody rootstock. Leaves 3-foliolate; leaflets ovate to lanceolate, hairy on lower veins, yellow-glandular on both surfaces. Flowers yellow, in axillary, long-stalked clusters. Pod ovate, softly hairy.

Ht: up to 90 cm. **Fl**: Nov–May. **Distr**: T.

Eriosema psoraleoides

Yellow-seed; Geelkeurtjie

Tall, erect, much-branched shrub, grey-hairy throughout. Leaves 3-foliolate. Flowers yellow, in dense terminal inflorescences. Pod flattish, dark brown, hairy, 2-seeded.

Ht: up to 2 m. **Fl**: Nov–Mar. **Distr**: N, W, C, E.

Eriosema salignum

Robust, erect perennial herb with grey-hairy stems from thick woody rootstock. Leaves 3-foliolate; leaflets silvery grey-hairy on undersurface, smooth above. Flowers yellow with red veins on outside of standard, orange inside.

Ht: up to 60 cm. **Fl**: Sep–Feb. **Distr**: T.

Eriosema simulans

Small, erect, perennial herb with shortly, silvery hairy stems from woody rootstock. Leaves 3-foliolate; leaflets elliptic, finely net-veined, silky hairy especially on veins and margins. Flowers yellow, in terminal, axillary raceme.

Fl: Sep–Feb. **Distr**: E, S.

Flemingia grahamiana

Much-branched, leafy shrub, softly hairy throughout. Leaves 3-foliolate; leaflets ovate, pointed, gland-dotted. Flowers yellow with reddish tinge, greenish white or pink, in dense axillary clusters.

Ht: up to 2.5 m. **Fl**: Jun–Aug. **Distr**: N, E.

OXALIDACEAE

Oxalis corniculata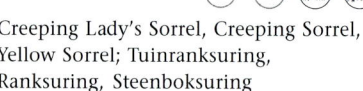

Creeping Lady's Sorrel, Creeping Sorrel, Yellow Sorrel; Tuinranksuring, Ranksuring, Steenboksuring

Creeping herb, with stolons and aerial stems from woody rootstock, often rooting at nodes. Leaves alternate, 3-foliolate; leaflets bright green, densely hairy below. Flowers 1–6, in axillary umbels, yellow. Fruit a 5-angled capsule.

Fl: Sep–Mar. **Distr**: T.

LINACEAE

Linum thunbergii

Small, erect, slightly shrubby, much-branched, smooth. Leaves opposite, pointed. Inflorescence branched, with shortly stalked, yellow flowers; sepals sharply pointed.

Ht: up to 40 cm. **Fl**: Oct–Jan. **Distr**: T.

ZYGOPHYLLACEAE

Tribulus terrestris

Dubbeltjie, Common Dubbeltjie; Dubbeltjie, Gewone-dubbeltjie

Much-branched, prostrate, annual herb with long, trailing, white-hairy stems. Leaves opposite, compound, with paired pinna, sparsely hairy above, white-hairy below. Flowers solitary, axillary, pale yellow.

Fl: Oct–Feb. **Distr**: T.

MALPIGHIACEAE

Sphedamnocarpus pruriens subsp. *pruriens*

Slender twiner with densely hairy stems. Leaves opposite or whorled, yellow-hairy on both surfaces; petiole with 2 stalked glands in upper half. Flowers few, axillary, pale yellow, with crinkled petals. Fruit reddish, with broad flat wings.
Fl: Dec–Mar. **Distr**: T.

EUPHORBIACEAE

Dalechampia capensis

Vigorous twiner or scrambler, thinly hairy throughout. Leaves deeply 3–5-lobed, margins slightly wavy. Flowers small, inconspicuous, surrounded by 3–5-lobed, cream-coloured or yellow, strongly veined floral bracts.

Fl: Sep–May. **Distr**: N, W, E.

Euphorbia striata var. *striata*
Milkweed, Milkwood, Spurge; Melkgras

Slender, erect, annual herb with unbranched, striate, smooth stem from woody rootstock. Leaves alternate, stem-clasping, narrowly linear, acute. Cyathia of 1 male and 1 female flower, yellow, enclosed in paired cup-shaped bracts, in 3–5 terminal panicles.

Ht: up to 50 cm. **Fl**: Oct–Nov. **Distr**: T.

TILIACEAE

Corchorus asplenifolius

Prostrate, perennial herb with trailing stems from woody rootstock. Leaves lanceolate, finely to coarsely toothed. Flowers small, star-shaped, yellow, axillary. Fruit a brown, sickle-shaped capsule.

Fl: Nov–Jan. **Distr**: T.

Triumfetta rhomboidea var. *rhomboidea*

Chinese Bur; Klitsbossie

Annual sometimes perennial, with erect stems stellate-hairy throughout. Leaves often 3-lobed, 3–7-nerved from base, irregularly toothed. Flowers yellow, star-shaped, in dense axillary clusters. Fruit small, globose, with many straight projections.

Ht: up to 2 m. **Fl**: Jul–Mar. **Distr**: N, W, E.

Triumfetta sonderi

Maagbossie, Spinnekopbossie, Waaierbossie

Erect, branched shrublet with slender stems, stellate-hairy throughout. Leaves ovate, alternate, margins shallowly toothed. Flowers small, star-shaped, yellow. Fruit globose, red, with long, rigid, bristly hairs.

Ht: up to 1 m. **Fl**: Nov–Mar. **Distr**: T.

Triumfetta welwitschii var. *welwitschii*

Erect herb with annual stems from perennial, woody rootstock. Leaves lanceolate, velvety on lower surface, velvety becoming smooth on upper surface, shortly toothed towards tip. Flowers yellow, in terminal clusters. Fruit globose, yellow-brown, with many long, bristled hairs.

Ht: up to 50 cm. **Fl**: Jul–Mar. **Distr**: N, E.

MALVACEAE

Abutilon angulatum var. *angulatum*

Erect, little-branched shrub, shortly velvety hairy. Leaves large, velvety, dark green above, paler below, with large basal sinus. Flowers yellow or orange, many at ends of lateral branches.

Ht: 1–3 m. **Fl**: Oct–Jun. **Distr**: N, W, C, S.

Sida cordifolia

Heartleaf Sida, Flannel Weed; Hartblaartaaiman

Soft shrub, closely, softly grey-velvety. Leaves heart-shaped at base, coarsely toothed. Flowers white, yellow or yellow-orange, in dense clusters at ends of branches.

Ht: up to 40 cm. **Fl**: Mar–Apr. **Distr**: N, W, C, E.

Sida dregei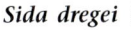

Spider-leg, Sutherland's Curse

Erect, much-branched, perennial herb, sparsely stellate-hairy. Leaves sharply toothed. Flowers orange to yellow, solitary on long slender stalks.

Ht: up to 40 cm. **Fl**: Dec–Mar. **Distr**: T.

Pavonia burchellii

Erect to spreading shrub. Leaves 3–5-lobed, with a deep basal sinus, margins coarsely toothed, hairy on both surfaces with star-shaped hairs. Flowers large, white, pale yellow, cream or orange, solitary, long-stalked.

Ht: up to 1 m. **Fl**: Oct–Mar. **Distr**: T.

Pavonia transvaalensis

Erect, weak, perennial herb, stellate-hairy throughout. Leaves long-stalked, 3–5-lobed, each lobe further lobed, dark green above, paler below. Calyx lobes long, narrow. Flowers pale yellow or white, solitary, axillary, long-stalked.

Ht: up to 50 cm. **Fl**: Mar–Apr. **Distr**: N, W, C.

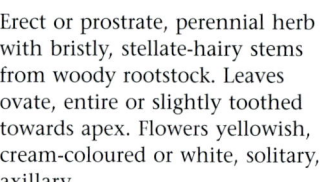

Hibiscus aethiopicus var. *ovatus*

Erect or prostrate, perennial herb with bristly, stellate-hairy stems from woody rootstock. Leaves ovate, entire or slightly toothed towards apex. Flowers yellowish, cream-coloured or white, solitary, axillary.

Ht: up to 35 cm. **Fl**: Oct–Jan. **Distr**: T.

Hibiscus calyphyllus

Hibiscus; Wildestokroos

Shrub or perennial herb with hairy stems becoming smooth later. Leaves stellate-hairy, 3–5-lobed, toothed. Flowers yellow with dark brown or reddish centre, solitary.

Ht: up to 3 m. **Fl**: Aug–Apr. **Distr**: T.

Hibiscus meeusei

Annual herb with semiwoody, stellate-hairy, erect stems branched from base. Leaves dark green, with purplish margin, 5-lobed or -angled. Flowers yellow with dark red centre, solitary.

Ht: up to 1 m. **Fl**: Feb–Mar. **Distr**: N, W, C, E.

STERCULIACEAE

Melhania prostrata

Robust, perennial herb or shrublet with prostrate or suberect, greyish brown-velvety stems from woody rootstock. Leaves 3-nerved at base, velvety, dotted with brown stellate hairs below. Flowers yellow, borne singly in upper axils.

Ht: up to 60 cm. **Fl**: Oct–Apr. **Distr**: T.

Hermannia grandistipula

Robust, erect, perennial herb or shrublet with much-branched stems from woody rootstock, stellate-hairy, velvety to the touch. Stipules large, deeply divided. Flowers yellow, mostly in axillary pairs.

Ht: up to 30 cm. **Fl**: Nov–Apr.
Distr: C, E, S, W.

Hermannia lancifolia

Small, erect to semi-erect herb from woody rootstock. Leaves grey-green, velvety, close to the ground, toothed towards tip. Flowers yellow or red, in 2-flowered cymes.

Ht: up to 25 cm. **Fl**: Oct–Mar. **Distr**: T.

Hermannia parvula

Slender, erect or prostrate perennial herb or shrublet, much-branched from woody rootstock. Leaves narrow, bright green, toothed. Flowers light yellow, cream-coloured or pink-red.

Ht: up to 10 cm. **Fl**: Sep–Feb.
Distr: C, W.

Hermannia transvaalensis

Prostrate herb with long, trailing stems, stellate-hairy throughout. Leaves broadly ovate, dark green with bronze tinge, margins bluntly toothed. Flowers yellow or apricot, in 2-flowered cymes.

Fl: Sep–Mar. **Distr**: C, E, S.

Waltheria indica

Meidebossie

Robust, erect herb with stellate-hairy, much-branched stems from woody base. Leaves ovate, irregularly toothed. Flowers yellow, small, in dense, axillary clusters.

Ht: up to 60 cm. **Fl**: Nov–Mar. **Distr**: N, W, C, E.

CLUSIACEAE

Hypericum aethiopicum subsp. *sonderi*

St John's Wort; Seeroogbossie

Perennial herb with erect, smooth stems, sometimes with black spots. Leaves sessile, opposite. Flowers yellow, red-tinged, distinctly veined, terminal, in few- to many-flowered inflorescences; stamens many.

Ht: up to 40 cm. **Fl**: Sep–Jan. **Distr**: T.

Hypericum revolutum

Curry Bush; Kerriebos

Tall, closely leafy shrub with stems often scaly-barked. Leaves opposite, sessile, with translucent glands. Flowers solitary, terminal, deep yellow, with stamens in 5 bundles of 20–30 each.

Ht: up to 4 m. **Fl**: Aug–Jan. **Distr**: N, E.

TURNERACEAE

Tricliceras longepedunculatum var. ***longepedunculatum***

Small, slender, erect, annual herb with dark red to purple, coarse, patent, scattered hairs. Leaves sessile, margins serrate. Flowers showy, bright orange outside, terminal.

Ht: up to 20 cm. **Fl**: Oct–Mar.
Distr: N, E.

BEGONIACEAE

Begonia sutherlandii
Wild Begonia

Perennial herb with thin, red, succulent stems from tuberous rootstock. Leaves unequal-sided, tapering to a point, lobed, sharply toothed, distinctly red-veined. Flowers terminal, orange.

Ht: up to 30 cm. **Fl**: Dec–Apr.
Distr: E, S.

THYMELAEACEAE

Gnidia caffra

Slender, little-branched shrublet with erect stems from woody rootstock. Leaves linear, well spaced. Flowers tubular, pale yellow, in terminal, few-flowered head.

Ht: up to 50 cm. **Fl**: Aug–May.
Distr: N, C, E, S.

Gnidia capitata
Gifbossie, Kerrieblom

Small, erect, branched shrublet, closely leafy. Leaves slightly hairy, pointed. Flowers tubular, yellow, compact in terminal, short-stalked, many-flowered inflorescences.

Ht: up to 30 cm. **Fl**: Jul–Feb. **Distr**: T.

Gnidia kraussiana var. ***kraussiana***
Gifbossie

Robust shrublet with erect, hairy stems from woody rootstock, forming small bushes. Leaves lance-shaped, pointed. Flowers tubular, yellow, silky hairy, arranged in dense, terminal flowerheads.

Ht: up to 50 cm. **Fl**: indefinite. **Distr**: T.

Gnidia microcephala
Balbossie, Besembos, Januariebos

Shrublet with erect, slender stems from woody rootstock. Leaves small, linear. Flowers few, small, tubular, orange-red, brown or yellow, silky hairy, in terminal flowerheads.

Ht: up to 50 cm. **Fl**: Sep–Feb.
Distr: W, C, E, S.

Gnidia sericocephala

Slender perennial with erect stems from woody rootstock. Leaves opposite, lance-shaped. Flowers tubular, pale yellow, silky hairy, in terminal, many-flowered, globose flowerheads.

Ht: up to 30 cm. **Fl**: Dec–May.
Distr: N, W, C, S.

Gnidia splendens

Many-stemmed, densely leafy shrublet. Leaves silvery hairy. Flowers tubular, pale yellow, in terminal flowerheads carried on stalks well beyond the leaves.

Ht: up to 40 cm. **Fl**: Jun–Dec. **Distr**: N, E.

ONAGRACEAE

Ludwigia octovalvis

Robust, well-branched herb, sometimes woody at base or even shrubby, with densely hairy stems from rootstock. Leaves conspicuously veined, hairy. Flowers yellow, axillary, long-stalked.

Ht: up to 4 m. **Fl**: Sep–Feb. **Distr**: W, S, E.

Oenothera glazioviana

Erect, branched, leafy shrublet. Leaves lanceolate, alternate, velvety hairy. Flowers large, long-stalked, yellow, terminal; calyx red-tinged.

Ht: up to 1 m. **Fl**: Jan–Apr. **Distr**: C, E.

Oenothera indecora
subsp. *indecora*

Evening Primrose; Nagblom

Erect, annual or biennial herb, much-branched from base, densely hairy. Leaves narrowly ovate, sessile, toothed, with reddish tinge. Flowers bright yellow fading reddish, opening near sunset.

Ht: up to 60 cm. **Fl**: Oct–Mar. **Distr**: T.

APIACEAE

Annesorrhiza flagellifolia

Slender, erect, smooth, perennial herb with underground rootstock covered with old leaf remains. Leaves few, basal, long-stalked, with opposite pairs of repeatedly divided leaflets. Male and female flowers on the same plant, yellow, in umbels.

Ht: up to 1 m. **Fl**: Sep–Nov.
Distr: N, E.

Peucedanum magalismontanum

Wild Parsley; Wildepieterselie

Erect, perennial herb with stem from strong taproot. Leaves repeatedly divided, with filiform lobes. Inflorescence a terminal, many-flowered umbel. Flowers small, yellow.

Ht: up to 1 m. **Fl**: Oct–Jan.
Distr: N, C, E, S.

OLEACEAE

Menodora africana

Balbossie

Small, erect, herbaceous undershrub with slender branches from woody base. Leaves deeply divided, alternate, or opposite to base. Flowers solitary, terminal, funnel-shaped, yellow, tinged brownish red outside.

Ht: up to 25 cm. **Fl**: Sep–Feb.
Distr: T.

GENTIANACEAE

Sebaea grandis

Small, slender erect, simple or branched herb. Leaves opposite. Flowers terminal, solitary or a few, tubular with spreading lobes, white, cream-coloured or yellow.

Ht: up to 35 cm. **Fl**: Jan–Mar.
Distr: T.

Sebaea macrophylla

Slender, erect herb branched from base. Leaves broadly ovate, opposite. Inflorescence dense, many-flowered, often leafy. Flowers yellow, tubular with spreading lobes.

Ht: up to 75 cm. **Fl**: Mar–Jul. **Distr**: E.

Sebaea sedoides var. *sedoides*

Erect or ascending, annual herb, much-branched from perennial rootstock. Leaves broadly ovate. Inflorescence a many-flowered panicle. Flowers yellow or rarely white, tubular with spreading lobes.

Ht: up to 65 cm. **Fl**: Jan–Mar. **Distr**: E, S.

MENYANTHACEAE

Nymphoides thunbergiana
Geelwateruintjie

Aquatic herb with short, erect rhizome. Leaves floating, leathery, orbicular, with deep basal sinus. Flowers star-shaped, yellow, with tufts of hairs on margin.

Fl: Sep–Jan. **Distr**: N, W, E, S.

APOCYNACEAE

Subfamily Asclepiadoideae

Asclepias aurea

Slender, erect, little-branched herb. Leaves small, linear, paired, with recurved margins. Inflorescence a terminal umbel of up to 4 yellow or white flowers.

Ht: up to 60 cm. **Fl**: Sep–Nov. **Distr**: T.

Sarcostemma viminale subsp. *viminale*

Caustic Bush, Caustic Creeper; Melkbos, Spantou, Melktou

Robust and vigorous climber with trailing or twining, succulent stems with milky latex. Leaves absent. Flowers small, cream-coloured or greenish yellow, in terminal or lateral clusters of up to 6 flowers. Follicles paired, green at first becoming brown, splitting to reveal silky hairy air-borne seeds.

Fl: Oct–Apr. **Distr**: T.

Orbeopsis lutea subsp. *lutea*

Succulent, leafless perennial with stems crowded, 4-angled, green, sometimes mottled with dull purple, toothed with stout acute teeth. Flowers star-shaped, with slender lobes, yellow, ciliate with purple club-shaped hairs.

Ht: up to 10 cm. **Fl**: Mar–Jun. **Distr**: N, W, C, E.

Tenaris chlorantha

Slender, erect herb with unbranched stem from tuberous rootstock. Leaves linear, opposite. Flowers axillary, star-shaped, yellow with red markings at throat.

Ht: up to 30 cm. **Fl**: Nov–Jan. **Distr**: C, S.

CONVOLVULACEAE

Merremia palmata

Smooth, prostrate or sometimes twining herb. Leaves deeply palmately 5–7-lobed; lobes linear. Inflorescence solitary. Flowers funnel-shaped, pale yellow with a deep red, maroon or deep magenta centre.

Fl: Nov–Apr. **Distr**: N, W, C, E.

Xenostegia tridentata subsp. *angustifolia*

Annual with smooth, rarely hairy, prostrate stems, sometimes twining. Leaves linear to narrowly oblong, with small basal teeth. Flowers small, funnel-shaped, with acute tips, pale yellow or dark yellow with dark reddish centre.

Fl: Feb. **Distr**: T.

Ipomoea obscura var. *obscura*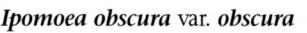
Wild Petunia; Wildepatat

Perennial with many slender, prostrate or twining, hairy or smooth stems from rootstock. Leaves heart-shaped, thinly hairy on both surfaces, margins ciliate, often wavy. Flowers broadly funnel-shaped, pale yellow.

Fl: Dec–Apr. **Distr**: T.

LAMIACEAE

Leonotis ocymifolia var. *schinzii*

Tall, erect shrub, much-branched from thick, woody base. Leaves stalked, ovate, velvety. Inflorescence of 2–5 spherical clusters of flowers. Flowers tubular, orange covered with orange-woolly hairs; calyx edged with sharp teeth.

Ht: 1–2 m. **Fl**: Dec–Apr. **Distr**: W, C, S.

SCROPHULARIACEAE

Manulea crassifolia subsp. ***crassifolia***

Robust, erect perennial herb with slightly downy stems from thick, woody rootstock. Basal leaves in rosette; stem leaves becoming smaller upwards. Flowers tubular, orange-yellow or red-brown.

Ht: up to 80 cm. **Fl**: Sep–Mar.
Distr: N, E, S.

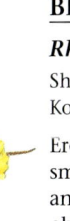

Striga elegans
Yellow flower colour form (see p. 194).

BIGNONIACEAE

Rhigozum brevispinosum
Short-thorn Pomegranate; Kortdoringgranaat

Erect, spiny, much-branched shrub or small tree. Spines straight, at right angle to stem. Leaves simple, oblanceolate, fascicled on short, dwarf lateral shoots below small spines. Flowers attractive, tubular, sweetly scented, golden yellow with reddish veins in throat.

Ht: up to 2 m. **Fl**: Sep–Dec.
Distr: N, W, E.

LENTIBULARIACEAE

Utricularia cf. ***arenaria***

Small, slender, erect, terrestrial herb. Stolons filiform, few to many from base of scape. Leaves many, obovate, 1-nerved. Traps many, on leaves and stolons. Inflorescence 1–5-flowered. Flowers white or lilac with yellow upper lip or sometimes with yellow blotch and darker purple markings on lower lip.

Ht: up to 10 cm. **Fl**: throughout the year.
Distr: T.

Utricularia stellaris
Bladderwort, Star Bladderwort; Sterblasiekruid

Small, aquatic herb. Stolons very long, filiform, sparsely branched. Leaves many, digitately divided into 3–6 rays. Bladders many, broadly ovoid. Inflorescence 2–16-flowered; axis arising below water surface, supported by ring 5 or 6 floats. Flowers yellow.

Ht: up to 30 cm. **Fl**: Feb–Jun. **Distr**: T.

ACANTHACEAE

Thunbergia atriplicifolia
Natal Primrose

Erect herb with several leafy, softly shaggy-hairy stems from woody rootstock. Leaves sessile or subsessile, opposite. Flowers terminal, usually solitary, large, tubular, cream-coloured to yellow, with pair of overlapping bracts clasping base.

Ht: up to 30 cm. **Fl**: Oct–Mar. **Distr**: T.

Justicia flava

Erect, perennial herb, slightly branched, thinly hairy throughout. Leaves ovate, in whorls. Inflorescence terminal, with successive flower clusters at short intervals. Flowers tubular, yellow.

Ht: up to 50 cm. **Fl**: Nov–May. **Distr**: N, W, C, E.

RUBIACEAE

Galium capense subsp. *garipense*

Much-branched perennial with erect or ascending stems covered with few recurved prickles, from woody rootstock. Leaves linear, in whorls of 6–8. Flowers small, yellow, creamy yellow or greenish yellow, in 3–many-flowered cymes at ends of branchlets.

Ht: up to 90 cm. **Fl**: Sep–Mar. **Distr**: C, S, W, E.

Rubia horrida

Weak-stemmed climber with 4-ribbed stems with recurved prickles. Leaves long-stalked, in whorls of 6–8. Flowers small, greenish yellow, in lax or dense inflorescences.

Ht: 2–3 m. **Fl**: Jan–Mar. **Distr**: T.

CUCURBITACEAE

Trochomeria debilis

Herbaceous climber on other plants, with smooth or hairy stems from tuberous rootstock. Leaves compound, deeply 5–7-lobed. Flowers axillary, both male and female greenish yellow. Fruit fleshy, ellipsoid, bright red when ripe.

Fl: Aug–Oct. **Distr**: T.

Coccinia adoensis
Wild Spinach; Bobbejaangif

Vigorous climber with slender, branched, hairy stems. Leaves deeply digitately 3–7-lobed, dark green above, paler below, shallowly toothed. Tendrils axillary, reddish. Flowers unisexual on the same plant; male flowers up to 12 together, yellow; female flowers small, yellow, solitary. Fruit ovoid, fleshy, turning orange when ripe.

Fl: Oct–Feb. **Distr**: T.

ASTERACEAE

Felicia mossamedensis

Somewhat shrubby, much-branched herb, roughly hairy throughout. Flowerheads solitary on long, slender stalks. Ray-florets yellow.

Ht: up to 40 cm. **Fl**: Oct–May. **Distr**: T.

Nidorella anomala

Slender, erect, closely leafy, perennial herb, thinly roughly hairy throughout. Leaves sessile, crowded. Florets yellow, in many, small, globose, compact flowerheads.

Ht: up to 60 cm. **Fl**: Dec–Mar. **Distr**: E, W, C, S.

Nidorella auriculata

Tall, robust, erect, single-stemmed, perennial herb, thinly roughly hairy throughout. Leaves sessile; base eared, stem-clasping; margins strongly toothed. Florets yellow, in many compact, terminal flowerheads.

Ht: 60–200 cm. **Fl**: Oct–May. **Distr**: T.

Nidorella hottentotica

Slender, erect, much-branched, perennial herb, white-tomentose throughout. Leaves sessile. Florets yellow, in many compact, terminal flowerheads.

Ht: up to 60 cm. **Fl**: Dec–Apr. **Distr**: T.

Nidorella resedifolia subsp. *resedifolia*

Stinkkruid, Wurmbossie

Annual herb with rough-hairy, leafy stems. Leaves simple, deeply divided, with 1 or 2 pairs of lobes. Florets bright yellow, in compact flowerheads.

Ht: up to 1 m. **Fl**: Sep–May. **Distr**: T.

Conyza aegyptica

Robust, erect, much-branched herb, thinly rough-hairy throughout. Leaves deeply divided. Florets pale yellow, in terminal, closely clustered flowerheads.

Ht: up to 80 cm. **Fl**: Dec–Feb.
Distr: N, E, W, C.

Conyza podocephala

Conyza; Bakbossie, Oondbos

Rough-hairy, perennial herb with tufted, erect or semi-erect, closely leafy stems, often reproducing by leafy runners. Basal leaves in a rosette. Florets yellow, in discoid flowerheads solitary on long stalks. Involucral bracts acuminate, glandular hairy.

Ht: up to 50 cm. **Fl**: Nov–Mar. **Distr**: E, W, C, S.

Nolletia rarifolia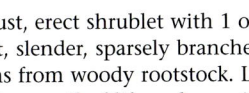

Robust, erect shrublet with 1 or few, erect, slender, sparsely branched, leafy stems from woody rootstock. Leaves erect, smooth, filiform becoming shorter upwards. Flowerheads solitary, terminal. Involucral bracts gland-dotted. Flowers yellow.

Ht: up to 30 cm. **Fl**: Oct–Feb. **Distr**: T.

Chrysocoma ciliata

Beesbossie, Brandbossie, Karoobossie

Bushy, twiggy shrublet with bare branches below, closely leafy upwards. Leaves alternate, linear, spreading or tips recurved, smooth, gland-dotted. Flowerheads solitary at ends of branchlets. Involucral bracts in 3 series, gland-dotted. Flowers bright yellow.

Ht: up to 1 m. **Fl**: Sep–May. **Distr**: W, C, E, S.

Achyrocline stenoptera

Erect or straggling, leafy, aromatic, perennial herb, smooth or white-woolly throughout. Leaves well spaced, narrow, tapering to a fine point. Inflorescence of loosely branched clusters. Involucral bracts bright yellow, in compact flowerheads.

Ht: ± 50 cm, sometimes 1.5 m.
Fl: Mar–Jun. **Distr**: T.

Helichrysum acutatum

Erect herb, much-branched from stout, woody rootstock, densely grey-woolly throughout. Leaves sessile, grey-woolly. Inflorescence terminal, compact, rounded. Involucral bracts bright yellow, in globose flowerheads.

Ht: up to 60 cm. **Fl**: Aug–Feb. **Distr**: T.

Helichrysum aureolum

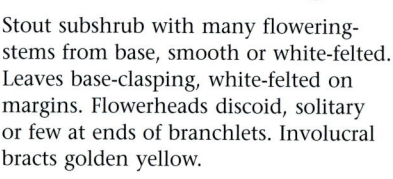

Stout subshrub with many flowering-stems from base, smooth or white-felted. Leaves base-clasping, white-felted on margins. Flowerheads discoid, solitary or few at ends of branchlets. Involucral bracts golden yellow.

Ht: up to 1 m. **Fl**: Feb–Jul. **Distr**: N, E.

Helichrysum aureonitens

Slender, erect, perennial herb with little-branched, whitish woolly stems from rhizome. Involucral bracts yellow, in terminal, globose flowerheads.

Ht: up to 30 cm. **Fl**: Sep–Feb. **Distr**: T.

Helichrysum aureum var. *monocephalum*

Slender, erect, perennial herb with simple flowering-stems from stout, woody rootstock, glandular-hairy, often thinly woolly. Leaves mostly basal, grey-white-woolly. Flowerheads discoid, usually solitary. Involucral bracts yellow.

Ht: up to 30 cm. **Fl**: Jul–Nov. **Distr**: T.

Helichrysum callicomum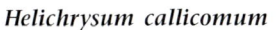

Many-stemmed, tufted, perennial herb, woody at base, closely leafy, densely white-felted throughout. Flowerheads small, slender, many in terminal clusters. Involucral bracts straw-coloured.

Ht: up to 40 cm. **Fl**: Feb–May **Distr**: T.

Helichrysum coriaceum

Teebossie, Vaalbossie

Tall, erect, perennial herb from woody rootstock, thinly white-felted. Leaves mostly basal, lanceolate, white-felted below. Involucral bracts straw-coloured, in terminal, globose flowerheads.

Ht: up to 70 cm. **Fl**: Oct–Jan. **Distr**: T.

Helichrysum mimetes

Erect shrublet, thinly greyish white-tomentose throughout. Leaves ovate with blade tapering to petiole-like base. Involucral bracts dull yellow, in terminal flowerheads.

Ht: up to 60 cm. **Fl**: May–Aug. **Distr**: N, E.

Helichrysum mundtii

Robust, erect, perennial herb from woody rootstock. Flowering-stem simple, branched in upper half, leafy, thinly white-felted. Leaves dark green on upper surface, pale green, velvety below. Flowerheads in terminal clusters. Involucral bracts creamy white to yellow.

Ht: up to 1.5 m. **Fl**: Feb–Apr. **Distr**: T.

Helichrysum nudifolium
Hottentot's Tea; Hottentotstee

Robust, erect, perennial herb. Flowering-stem simple, solitary, thinly woolly. Leaves large basally becoming smaller upwards, stem-clasping, prominently veined. Flowerheads many, in compact terminal clusters. Involucral bracts dull yellow.

Ht: up to 1.5 m. **Fl**: Oct–Apr. **Distr**: T.

Helichrysum obductum

Much-branched shrub with closely leafy, prostrate or erect, woody branchlets, grey-felted. Flowerheads bell-shaped, solitary or few together, in compact, terminal clusters. Involucral bracts yellow, glossy.

Ht: up to 60 cm. **Fl**: Apr–Oct, sometimes later. **Distr**: E.

Helichrysum odoratissimum

Hottentotskooigoed, Hottentotskooikruie

Much-branched, bushy, aromatic, perennial herb, thinly white-woolly throughout. Inflorescence terminal, branched, compact, rounded. Flowerheads many; involucral bracts bright or pale yellow.

Ht: up to 1.5 m. **Fl**: throughout the year. **Distr**: N, E, S.

Helichrysum oreophilum

Erect, perennial, closely leafy herb, much-branched from woody, branched rootstock, white-woolly throughout. Leaves becoming smaller upwards. Inflorescence terminal, compact, rounded. Involucral bracts lemon-yellow.

Ht: up to 30 cm. **Fl**: Sep–Dec. **Distr**: N, C, E, S.

Helichrysum pilosellum

Robust, perennial herb with erect, simple flowering-stem, white-felted, from stout tuberous rootstock. Leaves basal, few, ridged, densely white-felted below. Inflorescence rounded, branched. Florets pink or yellow surrounded by brownish bracts, in terminal, compact capitula.

Ht: up to 40 cm. **Fl**: Aug–Dec. **Distr**: T.

Helichrysum setosum

Robust, erect, perennial herb, much-branched, closely leafy, thinly hairy throughout. Leaves strap-shaped, stem-clasping. Involucral bracts bright yellow, in terminal flowerheads.

Ht: up to 60 cm. **Fl**: Jan–May. **Distr**: T.

Helichrysum splendidum

Virgate shrub, much-branched, closely leafy, grey-woolly, with leaf scar remains. Leaves grey-white-woolly, apex with stiff tip. Flowers yellow, surrounded by yellow, glossy involucral bracts, in terminal, compact flowerheads.

Ht: up to 1.5 m. **Fl**: Oct–Jan. **Distr**: E, S.

Pulicaria scabra

Annual herb with silky hairy, branched stems, becoming woody. Leaves sessile, stem-clasping, linear-oblong, decreasing in size upwards, entirely or shallowly toothed. Disc-florets yellow; ray-florets inconspicuous.

Ht: up to 1 m. **Fl**: Aug–Apr. **Distr**: T.

Geigeria burkei subsp. *burkei* var. *burkei*

Knoppiesvermeerbos, Vermeersiektebossie

Perennial herb with erect, leafy, woody stems often fork-branched. Leaves linear. Florets yellow, in solitary, sessile heads at forking of stems.

Ht: up to 60 cm. **Fl**: Dec–Jun. **Distr**: T.

Geigeria burkei subsp. *burkei* var. *hirtella*

Similar to var. *burkei* but differs in having scattered white or red, rough hairs throughout.

Ht: up to 40 cm. **Fl**: Sep–Mar. **Distr**: N, E, S.

Tridax procumbens
Tridax Daisy; Aster

Small, straggling, erect or prostrate, subwoody herb. Leaves opposite, deeply lobed. Florets pale yellow, in solitary, long-stalked, globose, terminal flowerheads.

Ht: up to 30 cm. **Fl**: May–Jul. **Distr**: N, E.

Phymaspermum acerosum
Geelblombos

Robust, erect, closely leafy, branched, aromatic shrub, thinly hairy. Leaves deeply divided, with linear lobes. Inflorescence dense, flat-topped or dome-shaped. Florets yellow, in many small, crowded flowerheads.

Ht: up to 60 cm. **Fl**: Apr–Jul. **Distr**: E.

Inezia integrifolia

Robust, erect, much-branched, closely leafy, perennial herb, hairy throughout. Leaves small, sessile. Florets yellow, in long-stalked, discoid flowerheads.

Ht: up to 60 cm. **Fl**: Nov–Mar. **Distr**: E.

Schistostephium artemisiifolium

Erect, much-branched, bushy herb from woody rootstock. Leaves deeply divided. Florets yellow in terminal, globose, compact flowerheads.

Ht: up to 50 cm. **Fl**: Dec–May. **Distr**: N, E.

Schistostephium crataegifolium
Bergkruie

Slender, erect, subwoody, leafy herb from stout, woody rootstock, long silky hairy throughout. Leaves deeply cut, with lobes often tipped by bristles. Florets yellow, in subsessile, globose flowerheads.

Ht: up to 75 cm. **Fl**: Jan–Apr. **Distr**: T.

Cineraria sp.
(= *C. fruticetorum* ined.)

Branched, straggling, closely leafy herb, sometimes trailing on other plants. Leaves deeply divided, white, downy on undersurface. Flowerheads in lax, terminal inflorescences. Florets yellow.

Ht: up to 1 m. **Fl**: Apr–Jul. **Distr**: N, E.

Senecio apiifolius

Slender, erect, annual herb, much-branched from base. Leaves deeply divided; lobes toothed. Florets yellow, in long-stalked, terminal, discoid heads.

Ht: up to 50 cm. **Fl**: throughout the year. **Distr**: N, W, C.

Senecio bupleuroides
Ragwort

Erect herb with slender, rigid, ribbed stems, woolly at base, smooth throughout. Leaves narrow, toothless, prominently veined. Flowerheads long-stalked, in loose inflorescences. Florets yellow.

Ht: up to 75 cm. **Fl**: Sep–Dec. **Distr**: E, S.

Senecio coronatus
Sybossie

Robust, perennial herb with rigid, erect, hairy stems, white-woolly at base. Leaves few, ovate, mostly basal. Flowerheads solitary or few. Florets yellow.

Ht: up to 75 cm. **Fl**: Sep–Dec. **Distr**: T.

Senecio gregatus

Rigid, erect, single-stemmed, closely leafy herb, smooth or finely downy throughout. Leaves sharply toothed. Inflorescence a compact, dome-shaped cluster of many small, scented flowerheads. Florets yellow.

Ht: up to 75 cm. **Fl**: Apr–May. **Distr**: W, C, S, E.

Senecio inaequidens

Canary Weed; Geelopslag

Perennial, erect, closely leafy herb, much-branched from base. Flowerheads few to many in terminal, open inflorescences. Ray-and disc-florets bright yellow.

Ht: up to 1 m. **Fl**: Oct–Feb, sometimes later. **Distr**: N, E, S.

Senecio inornatus

Erect, perennial herb, few-stemmed from woody rootstock. Leaves elongated, shortly toothed. Florets bright yellow, in flat-topped, sessile flowerheads.

Ht: up to 1.8 m. **Fl**: Dec–Mar. **Distr**: T.

Senecio laevigatus var. *integrifolius*

Small, erect, annual herb, much-branched from woody base. Leaves narrow, linear, mostly basal. Flowers yellow, in globose, long-stalked, terminal flowerheads.

Ht: up to 30 cm. **Fl**: Sep–Mar. **Distr**: C, S.

Senecio lydenburgensis

Slender, erect, perennial herb from thick, woody rootstock, crowned with coarse leaf bases. Flowerheads up to 40, terminal. Florets bright yellow.

Ht: up to 1 m. **Fl**: Dec–Feb. **Distr**: E, W, C, S.

Senecio microglossus
Cape Ivy

Small, much-branched, closely leafy, twiggy shrub, smooth throughout. Leaves lanceolate, margins sharply toothed. Flowerheads terminal, in small clusters. Florets yellow.

Ht: up to 1 m. **Fl**: Oct–Jan, sometimes later. **Distr**: E.

Senecio oxyriifolius

Fleshy, perennial herb with slender, erect flowering-stem from creeping, tuberous rootstock. Leaves fleshy, variable in shape from orbicular to deltoid, toothed. Florets bright yellow, in discoid, terminal flowerheads.

Ht: up to 1 m. **Fl**: Sep–Jan. **Distr**: T.

Senecio pleistocephalus

Branched, somewhat succulent, scandent shrub with weak, smooth, leafy stems. Leaves elliptic, acute, entire or toothed. Inflorescence discoid. Florets bright yellow.

Fl: Apr–Jul. **Distr**: N, W, E, C.

Senecio venosus

Besembossie

Erect, perennial, closely leafy herb, woolly throughout. Leaves simple, sessile, prominently veined. Flowerheads many, in long-stalked branched inflorescences. Florets bright yellow.

Ht: up to 75 cm. **Fl**: Nov–Jan, sometimes after burning. **Distr**: T.

Euryops pedunculatus

Robust, erect, much-branched, closely leafy shrublet. Leaves alternate, deeply divided; lobes linear. Flowerheads solitary, long-stalked at ends of branchlets. Ray-florets yellow.

Ht: up to 1 m. **Fl**: Aug–Apr. **Distr**: N, W, E, S.

Oligocarpus calendulaceus

(⇐ *Osteospermum calendulaceum*)

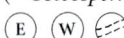

Strong-smelling, annual herb with several prostrate or ascending, leafy, glandular-hairy stems from base. Leaves long-stalked at base. Florets yellow, in solitary flowerheads in axils of upper leaves.

Fl: Jul–Sep. **Distr**: C.

Osteospermum striatum

Small, erect, perennial herb with many leafy stems from thick, woody rootstock. Flowerheads terminal, solitary, stalked. Ray-florets bright yellow.

Ht: up to 10 cm. **Fl**: Oct–Apr, sometimes later. **Distr**: E.

Ursinia nana subsp. *leptophylla*

Slender, erect, branched annual herb. Leaves deeply divided; lobes linear. Flowerheads terminal, solitary, on long stalks. Ray-florets yellow.

Ht: up to 40 cm. **Fl**: Dec–Mar. **Distr**: T.

Haplocarpha scaposa

Bietou, Tontelbossie

Stemless, perennial herb. Leaves 4 or 5, prostrate, in a basal rosette, densely hairy on upper surface, white-felted below. Flowerheads solitary, terminal, on stout stalks. Ray-florets yellow; disc-florets yellow.

Ht: up to 30 cm. **Fl**: Sep–Mar. **Distr**: T.

Hirpicium bechuanense

Small, slender, erect, perennial herb with bristly-hairy stems. Leaves grey-green above, white-felted below, margins sharply toothed, with bristly hairs. Flowerheads terminal, solitary. Florets yellow.

Fl: Jan–Mar. **Distr**: N, W, C, E. **Ht**: up to 30 cm.

Berkheya insignis

Perennial herb with simple, softly hairy, leafy stems from stout, woody rootstock. Leaves sessile, sharply bristled along margins, white-felted below. Flowerheads solitary. Involucral bracts linear, spiny. Florets golden yellow.

Ht: up to 50 cm. **Fl**: Aug–Dec. **Distr**: T.

Berkheya pinnatifida subsp. *ingrata*

Robust, erect, perennial herb or subshrub with thinly hairy stems. Leaves sessile, rigid, deeply lobed; lobes up to 10 pairs, spiny, margins bristly, hairy on both surfaces. Flowerheads discoid. Flowers yellow, surrounded by spiny bracts.

Ht: up to 50 cm. **Fl:** Dec–Mar. **Distr:** W, C, E, S.

Berkheya radula
Boesmanrietjie

Robust, erect, perennial herb with short, prickly stems from thick, woody rootstock. Leaves basal, large, deeply lobed, edged with prickles, white-felted below. Flowerheads solitary on short stalks. Ray-florets pale yellow.

Ht: up to 1 m. **Fl:** Oct–Dec, sometimes later. **Distr:** T.

Berkheya setifera
Rasperdissel

Perennial, erect herb from stout, woody rootstock, roughly hairy. Leaves few, coarsely, shallowly toothed, spiny. Involucral bracts spiny. Florets bright golden yellow.

Ht: up to 1.2 m. **Fl:** Sep–Feb. **Distr:** N, E, S.

Gerbera piloselloides
(= *Piloselloides hirsuta*)

Stemless, perennial herb, hairy throughout. Leaves many, basal, subsessile. Flowerheads solitary, on erect flowering stalk. Florets white, pink or yellow.

Ht: up to 30 cm. **Fl**: Jul–Feb. **Distr**: T.

Hypochoeris radicata
Hairy Wild Lettuce; Harige-skaapslaai

Stemless, perennial herb with stout rootstock. Leaves in a basal rosette, lobed. Flowerheads solitary, at ends of long inflorescence branches. Florets yellow.

Ht: up to 60 cm. **Fl**: Sep–Mar. **Distr**: N, E, S.

Taraxacum breviscapum

Small, stemless, perennial herb. Leaves in a basal rosette, deeply 4- or 5-lobed; lobes triangular, toothed; stalk and midrib purplish. Florets yellow, solitary, in long-stalked flowerheads.

Ht: up to 30 cm. **Fl**: May–Oct. **Distr**: C, S, W.

Blue Flowers

COMMELINACEAE

Commelina benghalensis

Blouselblommetjie

Robust, much-branched, ± succulent herb with smooth or thinly hairy stems from thin roots. Leaves stem-clasping, broadly ovate. Flowers pale blue, protruding from a folded spathe.

Ht: up to 30 cm. **Fl**: Oct–Jan. **Distr**: T.

Commelina eckloniana

Slender, trailing herb with thinly hairy, annual stems from rootstock. Leaves with sheathing base. Flowers pale blue, from stalked spathes.

Ht: up to 60 cm. **Fl**: Oct–Feb. **Distr**: T.

Commelina erecta

Erect or spreading, perennial herb, rooting at nodes. Flowers blue, with single spathe. Fruit capsule with dorsal locule indehiscent, tuberculate.

Ht: up to 50 cm. **Fl**: Dec–Apr. **Distr**: N, W, C, E.

Commelina livingstonii

Slender herb with spreading, jointed stems and sheathing grey-green leaves. Flowers pale blue fading in midmorning.

Ht: up to 50 cm.
Fl: Oct–Feb. **Distr**: T.

Cyanotis speciosa

Doll's Powder-Puff; Bloupoeierkwassie

Slender, erect, perennial herb. Leaves in basal rosettes. Flowers mauve to pale blue; anthers bright yellow; filaments bearded with hairs giving them a woolly look.

Ht: up to 60 cm. **Fl**: Oct–Apr. **Distr**: T.

AGAPANTHACEAE

Agapanthus inapertus subsp. *inapertus*

Tall, erect, perennial herb, growing in tight groups. Leaves 6–8, basal, strap-shaped, channelled. Inflorescence a long-stalked, many-flowered umbel. Flowers tubular, pendulous, violet or deep blue; styles exserted.

Ht: up to 1 m. **Fl**: Jan–Mar.
Distr: N, C, E.

HYACINTHACEAE

Scilla natalensis

Wild Squill, Blue Hyacinth; Blouslangkop

Tall, robust, erect, herbaceous geophyte with flowering-stem from large bulb covered with many rows of reddish brown tunics. Leaves 6–8, basal, hairy or smooth. Flowering-stem purple. Flowers bright blue to pale mauve.

Ht: up to 50 cm. **Fl**: Sep–Oct. **Distr**: N, C, E, S.

IRIDACEAE

Aristea woodii

Slender to robust plant. Basal leaves 2–14, linear, margins green-brown. Cauline leaves 1–11, linear, bases keeled. Flowers dark blue, pale blue or deep mauve.

Ht: up to 1.4 m. **Fl**: Nov–Feb. **Distr**: T.

Lapeirousia sandersonii
Blou-Angelier

Slender, erect flowering-stem and leaves from corm with brown, membranous tunic, deep underground, neck covered by brown bracts. Leaves linear, ± 4. Inflorescence 8–12, branched. Flowers tubular, blue or mauve, with darker markings on inner lobes.

Ht: up to 30 cm. **Fl**: Jan–Mar. **Distr**: N, W, C.

ORCHIDACEAE

Herschelianthe baurii

Slender, erect herb with stems from tuberous rootstock. Leaves slender, grass-like, sheathing at base, appearing after flowering time. Flowers attractive, sky-blue to purple-blue, 2–14, terminal.

Ht: up to 40 cm. **Fl**: Sep–Oct. **Distr**: N, E, S.

NYMPHAEACEAE

Nymphaea nouchali var. ***caerulea***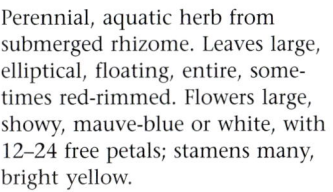

Waterlily; Blouwaterlelie

Perennial, aquatic herb from submerged rhizome. Leaves large, elliptical, floating, entire, sometimes red-rimmed. Flowers large, showy, mauve-blue or white, with 12–24 free petals; stamens many, bright yellow.

Ht: ± 50 cm or depending on depth of water. **Fl**: Sep–Mar. **Distr**: T.

CONVOLVULACEAE

Evolvulus alsinoides

Small, perennial herb with few to several, slender, erect or decumbent, densely hairy stems. Leaves simple, ovate, subsessile. Flowers light blue, sometimes white.

Ht: up to 30 cm. **Fl**: Dec–Apr. **Distr**: W, C, E, S.

BORAGINACEAE

Cynoglossum austroafricanum

Robust, erect, perennial herb with several roughly hairy stems from base. Leaves alternate, elliptic, hairy. Flowers small, tubular, bright blue in dense, terminal clusters.

Ht: up to 1 m. **Fl**: Nov–Feb. **Distr**: C.

VERBENACEAE

***Clerodendrum triphyllum*
var. *triphyllum***

Small shrublet with erect to semi-erect, unbranched stems from woody rootstock, thinly hairy throughout. Leaves mostly in threes, sessile. Flowers showy, axillary, deep blue, lobed; lower lobe larger than upper four.

Ht: up to 50 cm. **Fl**: Sep–Jan. **Distr**: T.

LAMIACEAE

Salvia runcinata

Erect, perennial herb with 1–many hairy, gland-dotted stems from creeping rootstock. Leaves subsessile, deeply divided; lobes further irregularly divided, hairy. Flowers tubular, white or pale blue to mauve or purplish, in many rows.

Ht: up to 50 cm. **Fl**: Oct–Mar. **Distr**: T.

Salvia tiliifolia

Annual herb with simple or branched, sparsely hairy stems. Leaves stalked, ovate, sparsely hairy. Inflorescence simple, with many rows of 6–14 flowers. Flowers tubular, blue.

Ht: up to 60 cm. **Fl**: Apr–Jun. **Distr**: C.

Pycnostachys reticulata

Tall, erect, perennial herb, hairy throughout. Leaves sessile, opposite, margins finely toothed. Inflorescence solitary or several together, many-flowered; bracts linear. Flowers pale blue to mauve to pink; calyx teeth 5, spiny.

Ht: up to 2 m. **Fl**: Jan–Apr. **Distr**: T.

Solenostemon latifolius

Perennial herb with semi-erect to procumbent, hairy stems. Leaves thick in texture, hairy, sometimes with dark V-shaped blotch on upper surface, red gland-dotted on lower surface. Flowers tubular, violet to purple, gland-dotted.

Ht: up to 50 cm. **Fl**: Mar–Aug. **Distr**: N, E.

SCROPHULARIACEAE

Aptosimum lineare

Small herb with many stems growing close to the ground, from long rootstock. Leaves narrow, long, silky hairy at base, forming leaf remains on dying. Flowers tubular, deep blue or purple.

Ht: up to 30 cm. **Fl**: Aug–Feb. **Distr**: N, C, E.

Craterostigma plantagineum

Small, erect, perennial herb. Leaves broadly ovate, 4 or 5 in a basal rosette, conspicuously veined. Flowers white with bright blue markings and two orange spots at the throat.

Ht: up to 10 cm. **Fl**: Dec–Mar. **Distr**: N, W, C, E.

Lindernia wilmsii

Small, slender, erect, annual, much-branched herb. Leaves small, linear. Flowers small, terminal, solitary, tubular, white or blue, with purple tip.

Ht: up to 10 cm. **Fl**: Dec–Apr. **Distr**: E.

ACANTHACEAE
Barleria obtusa

Barleria, Bush-violet, South Coast Bush-violet

Tall, erect, perennial herb with slender, irregularly much-branched stems becoming woody, thickly hairy throughout. Leaves subsessile, opposite, ovate. Flowers large, trumpet-shaped, with spreading lobes, blue, purple or white, crowded at ends of branches.

Ht: up to 1 m. **Fl**: Mar–May. **Distr**: T.

Blepharis saxatilis

Prostrate to semi-erect shrublet with stems from woody rootstock. Leaves lanceolate, opposite, spiny. Flowers 5-cleft, blue, conspicuously veined, hairy at throat, surrounded by large, shiny, spiny bracts.

Ht: up to 30 cm. **Fl**: Apr–May. **Distr**: N, W, C, E.

RUBIACEAE
Pentanisia angustifolia

Erect, perennial herb with stems branched from woody rootstock. Leaves sessile, in whorls. Flowers tubular, pale blue to lilac, in long-stalked heads.

Ht: up to 50 cm. **Fl**: Aug–Jan. **Distr**: T.

Pentanisia prunelloides
subsp. *prunelloides*

Robust, erect herb with densely hairy stems from woody rootstock. Leaves 3 times longer than broad. Inflorescence dense, many-flowered, long-stalked. Flowers tubular, blue, hairy.

Ht: up to 60 cm. **Fl**: Oct–Mar. **Distr**: T.

CAMPANULACEAE

Wahlenbergia undulata

Pale Bluebell

Slender, erect, much-branched, perennial herb with scattered white hairs, especially on leaves. Leaves mostly in lower half, sessile, with wavy margins. Flowers bell-shaped, purple, blue, white or yellow.

Ht: up to 60 cm. **Fl**: Jan–Apr. **Distr**: T.

LOBELIACEAE

Lobelia flaccida subsp. *flaccida*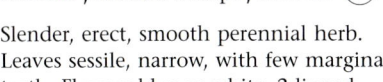

Slender, erect, smooth perennial herb. Leaves sessile, narrow, with few marginal teeth. Flowers blue or white, 2-lipped; lower lip much larger than upper.

Ht: up to 30 cm. **Fl**: Sep–Jun. **Distr**: T.

Lobelia flaccida subsp. *mossiana*

Differs from subsp. *flaccida* by the inverted, top-shaped calyx, the sharply serrate lower leaves, the somewhat broader leaves and narrow stem wings.

Ht: up to 30 cm. **Fl**: Dec–May. **Distr**: N, C, E, S.

Monopsis decipiens

Slender, erect herb with single stem from creeping rhizome. Leaves small, alternate, sessile, narrowly lanceolate. Flowers 1–3, terminal at end of stems, 2-lipped, lower lip bright blue with two bright yellow spots near base, 3-lobed, upper lip 2-lobed, purplish blue.

Ht: up to 20 cm. **Fl**: Dec–Mar. **Distr**: T.

ASTERACEAE

Ageratum houstonianum

Garden Ageratum; Tuin-ageratum

Robust, erect, annual herb, softly hairy throughout. Leaves opposite, ovate, margins toothed. Flowerheads small, globose, in terminal clusters. Florets blue.

Ht: up to 1 m. **Fl**: Jun–Dec. **Distr**: N, W, E.

Senecio gerrardii

Robust, erect herb, aromatic, glandular, often sticky. Leaves large, divided, with large teeth on margins. Inflorescence terminal, much-branched. Flowerheads in dense, rounded clusters. Florets deep purplish blue.

Ht: up to 1 m. **Fl**: Jan–Apr. **Distr**: W, E, S.

Lactuca inermis
(= *L. capensis*)

Tall, erect, perennial herb with smooth, spreading, much-branched stems from thick, woody rootstock. Leaves irregularly toothed. Flowers white or bluish, rarely yellow, in axillary flowerheads.

Ht: up to 30 cm. **Fl**: throughout the year. **Distr**: T.

Mauve/Purple Flowers

COMMELINACEAE
Aneilema hockii

Slender herb with procumbent or ascending stems, thinly covered with white, hooked hairs, rough to the touch. Flowers with 3 pale mauve petals.

Ht: up to 60 cm. **Fl**: Dec–Feb. **Distr**: T.

Cyanotis lapidosa

Perennial herb with many slender, purple, zigzag spreading stems. Leaves fleshy, hairy, alternate; lower leaves in a basal rosette. Inflorescence compact, sessile, axillary, terminal. Flowers purple to mauve to bright magenta, with hairs giving flowers a woolly appearance; stamens bright yellow.

Ht: up to 30 cm. **Fl**: Jan–Mar. **Distr**: T.

Floscopa glomerata

Slender, soft-stemmed, erect, perennial, aquatic herb, exserted above water level, often rooting at lower nodes. Flowers small, mauve, glandular-hairy, in dense, terminal clusters.

Ht: 30–60 cm. **Fl**: Feb–May. **Distr**: T.

ALLIACEAE

Tulbaghia acutiloba

Perennial herb with slender flowering-stem from short, thickened, fleshy, bulb-like rootstock. Plants smelling strongly of garlic when bruised. Leaves basal, grass-like. Flowers with greenish purple tepals and orange corona, sweetly scented.

Ht: up to 20 cm. **Fl:** Aug–Apr, especially after fires. **Distr:** W, C, E, S.

HYACINTHACEAE

Ledebouria cooperi
Cooper's Squill

Small, erect, herbaceous geophyte with globose bulb covered with few membranous scales. Leaves 1–3, fleshy, erect. Inflorescence a simple, up to 50-flowered raceme. Flowers lilac to bright purple.

Ht: up to 10 cm. **Fl:** Sep–Jan. **Distr:** T.

Ledebouria revoluta

Small, erect, herbaceous geophyte with broad, strap-shaped leaves and several flowering-stems from large, globose bulb covered with tunic layers. Leaves purple-spotted. Flowers green with brownish purple markings; anthers purple.

Ht: up to 20 cm. **Fl:** Oct–Feb. **Distr:** T.

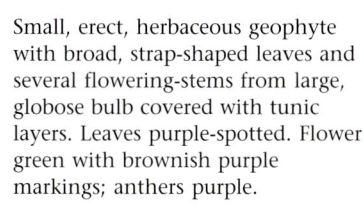

VELLOZIACEAE

Xerophyta humilis
(formerly *Vellozia*)

Small, low-growing, trailing or mat-forming, fibrous perennial. Leaves linear-lanceolate, flat, densely tufted, terminal. Flowers mauve, long-stalked; flowering-stem glandular.

Ht: up to 10 cm. **Fl:** Jan–Apr. **Distr:** N, W, C, E.

Xerophyta retinervis

Monkey's Tail; Bobbejaanstert, Olifantstert, Besembos

Erect, fibrous perennial with conspicuous, dwarf tufted stems irregularly branched, covered by thick leaf bases. Leaves linear-lanceolate, in terminal tufts. Flowers showy, solitary, pale to deep mauve, slender-stalked, borne between leaves; anthers orange-yellow.

Ht: up to 50 cm. **Fl**: any season, especially after fires. **Distr**: W, C, E.

IRIDACEAE

Moraea thomsonii

Small, erect, branched, herbaceous perennial, from globose corm with tunic of coarse, dark brown fibres. Leaf solitary, absent at flowering time. Spathe dry, papery. Flowers pale lilac to mauve, with yellow nectar guides.

Ht: up to 30 cm. **Fl**: Aug–Sep. **Distr**: E.

Dierama galpinii

Slender, erect geophyte with flowering-stem from corm covered with long bristles. Leaves 3, erect, finely ribbed. Flowers maroon, dark mauve, red, magenta, 7–12 on long, slender, stalked spikes.

Ht: up to 1.2 m. **Fl**: Oct–Jan. **Distr**: T.

Babiana hypogea var. *hypogea*

Bobbejaanuintjie, Ertappeluintjie

Small, erect herb with flowering-stem and leaves from large, globose corm covered with tunic of red-brown, fibrous layers. Leaves grass-like. Flowers funnel-shaped, mauve, sweetly scented, crowded at base.

Ht: up to 30 cm. **Fl**: Feb–Apr. **Distr**: T.

Gladiolus elliotii

Tall, erect plant with globose, depressed corm with brown, fibrous tunic. Leaves 7, base-clasping, with yellow midrib. Flowers mauve, blue or white, densely speckled with maroon, purple or pink spots, in dense spikes.

Ht: up to 80 cm. **Fl**: Nov–May. **Distr**: T.

Gladiolus papilio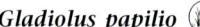

Attractive, erect plant, with simple flowering-stems from subglobose corm with reddish brown tunic. Leaves lance-shaped, 7 or 8. Inflorescence a lax spike of 5–10 flowers. Flowers funnel-shaped, varying from yellow tinged with mauve or dull purple to purple with darker markings.

Ht: up to 80 cm. **Fl**: Dec–Mar. **Distr**: T.

Gladiolus permeabilis subsp. *edulis*

Aandblommetjie

Erect plants growing solitary from subglobose corm with coarse brown fibres. Leaves at base with membranous sheaths, erect. Flowers tubular, with lobes cordate, spreading, white to cream-coloured, sometimes tinged mauve, pink or grey, often with deep pink, crimson or purplish median line.

Ht: up to 50 cm. **Fl**: throughout the year. **Distr**: T.

Gladiolus pretoriensis

Erect plant growing solitary from ovoid corm with tunic of coarse, brown, parallel fibres. Leaves 3 or 4, inrolled. Inflorescence an unbranched, 4–9-flowered spike. Flowers purple or pink, the lower side lobes with yellow eye outlined with purple.

Ht: up to 50 cm. **Fl**: Feb–Mar.
Distr: W, C, S.

ORCHIDACEAE

Stenoglottis fimbriata

Small, erect, perennial herb with slender, purple flowering-stem from succulent, tuberous roots. Leaves 5–20, basal, sometimes spotted with purple, margins wavy. Flowers small, lilac with darker spots; lip 3-lobed.

Ht: up to 30 cm.
Fl: Jan–Mar. **Distr**: E.

Eulophia clavicornis var. *clavicornis*

Slender, erect, terrestrial herb with subterranean, moniliform rhizome. Leaves simple, basal. Inflorescence 3–18-flowered. Flowers from purple to white to yellow; petals fused into a column.

Ht: up to 90 cm. **Fl**: Aug–Oct. **Distr**: T.

NYCTAGINACEAE

Commicarpus pentandrus

Veldpatat

Robust, sprawling, perennial herb, slightly hairy throughout. Leaves subsessile, margins irregular, bearing one or more small points. Flowers funnel-shaped, magenta or pinkish purple; style exserted.

Fl: indefinite. **Distr**: T.

RANUNCULACEAE

Clematopsis scabiosifolia
subsp. ***stanleyi***

Wild Dog; Pluimbossie, Veerbossie

Robust, erect, perennial herb, hairy throughout. Leaves deeply divided, each lobe further divided. Flowers large, cream-coloured, white, pale pink or purple, sweetly scented. Fruit a compact aggregate of achenes each crowned with persistent feathery styles.

Ht: up to 50 cm. **Fl**: Dec–Mar. **Distr**: C, S, W.

FABACEAE

Tephrosia longipes
subsp. ***longipes***

Stiffly erect, perennial herb with slightly hairy stems from woody rootstock. Leaves compound, with 3 or 4 pairs of opposite leaflets and a terminal one. Flowers pink or purple.

Ht: up to 90 cm. **Fl**: Dec–Apr. **Distr**: T.

Tephrosia rhodesica

Robust, erect, much-branched herb or shrublet with light to rusty brown-hairy stems. Leaves compound, with 5–9 ovate leaflets, densely hairy on undersurface. Flowers purple, in dense, terminal raceme; style not twisted.

Ht: up to 70 cm. **Fl**: Dec–Mar. **Distr**: T.

Neorautanenia ficifolius

Blou-ertjie

Long, trailing herb with annual, decumbent stems from perennial rootstock. Leaves 3-foliolate; leaflets deeply divided into 5 lobes; middle lobe larger than the rest. Flowers bright blue-purple, in axillary clusters.

Fl: Nov–Jan. **Distr**: T.

Vigna frutescens subsp. *frutescens* var. *frutescens*

Robust straggler or climber on other plants, from woody rootstock. Leaves 3-foliolate; leaflets with distinct pale green mark along midrib. Flowers few at ends of long stalks, purple.

Fl: Nov–Feb. **Distr**: T.

Vigna vexillata var. *vexillata*

Wild-cowpea, Wild Sweetpea; Wilde-ertjie

Perennial climber on other plants, with slender, hairy stems from woody rootstock. Leaves 3-foliolate. Flowers 2–6, at ends of long stalks, white, mauve or pale pink, ageing to yellow.

Fl: Jan–Apr. **Distr**: T.

Lablab purpureus subsp. *uncinatus*

Perennial climber with slender, shortly hairy stems. Leaves 3-foliolate; leaflets ovate-triangular. Flowers purple or cream-coloured tinged mauve outside and purple inside, axillary. Pods oblong-sickle-shaped, flat, with nodules along upper or both margins.

Fl: Jan–Apr. **Distr**: N, W, C, E.

GERANIACEAE

Geranium multisectum

Perennial herb with slender, well-branched, sprawling, hairy stems. Stipules deeply dissected. Leaves digitately lobed to base, each lobe further divided, densely white-hairy below. Flowers violet, purple or magenta.

Ht: up to 30 cm. **Fl**: Sep–Feb. **Distr**: E, S.

MALPIGHIACEAE

Triaspis hypericoides subsp. ***nelsonii***

Scandent shrub with twining stems, sometimes erect. Leaves ovate, 1–3 times longer than wide, smooth to densely white-hairy. Flowers lilac fading to white. Fruit winged, green ripening to pale brown.

Ht: up to 1.5 m. **Fl:** Oct–May.
Distr: W, C, E, S.

POLYGALACEAE

Polygala amatymbica

Dwarf, perennial herb with woody rootstock. Leaves ovate. Flowers deep purple, solitary or few together, axillary.

Ht: up to 15 cm. **Fl:** Sep–Dec.
Distr: T.

Polygala hottentotta

Slender, erect, perennial herb with little-branched stems from woody rootstock. Leaves simple, lance-shaped. Flowers dark purple, in some parts pale purple and others veined green, in terminal raceme.

Ht: up to 60 cm. **Fl:** Nov–Feb. **Distr:** T.

Polygala uncinata

Perennial herb with slender, erect, annual stems from woody rootstock. Leaves lance-shaped, alternate. Flowers deep purple, winged, in terminal, few-flowered raceme.

Ht: up to 60 cm. **Fl**: Oct–Mar. **Distr**: T.

Polygala virgata var. *decora*

Bloukappie

Slender, erect, little-branched shrub. Leaves simple, linear to elliptic, hairy at first becoming smooth. Flowers large for the genus, deep purple to pale lilac, partly veined green.

Ht: up to 3 m. **Fl**: Oct–Feb. **Distr**: T.

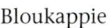

MALVACEAE

Hibiscus microcarpus

Small dwarf shrub with spreading stems. Leaves narrow, stellate-hairy on margins. Flowers large, yellow or purple with dark red centre, solitary.

Ht: up to 30 cm. **Fl**: Nov–Apr. **Distr**: W, C, S.

STERCULIACEAE

Hermannia coccocarpa

Small, robust, erect herb, much-branched from woody rootstock. Leaves slender-stalked, sharply toothed. Flowers mauve, purple or pink, in terminal 2-flowered cymes.

Ht: up to 20 cm. **Fl**: Jul–Mar. **Distr**: C, S, W, E.

VIOLACEAE

Hybanthus enneaspermus
Pink Lady's-slipper

Small, erect, annual herb with several branched stems from woody rootstock. Leaves scattered, lanceolate, slightly toothed. Flowers axillary, solitary, pale bluish mauve or yellow, with unequal petals, the lower larger and differing in shape from the rest.

Ht: up to 30 cm. **Fl**: Oct–Jan. **Distr**: N, C, E.

MELASTOMATACEAE

Dissotis canescens
Ordeal Bean, Wild Lasiandra

Tall, erect, much-branched shrub, grey-velvety throughout. Leaves opposite, ovate, distinctly 5-veined from base, hairy. Flowers sweetly scented, showy, pink to purple to red, with conspicuous stamens.

Ht: up to 1.2 m. **Fl**: Jan–Apr. **Distr**: N, E, S.

Antherotoma phaeotricha

Slender, erect herb, with much-branched, reddish brown, rough, long-hairy stems from thick, tuberous rhizome. Leaves opposite, 3-veined, dark green above, paler below. Flowers terminal, pink, mauve-pink or purple.

Ht: up to 40 cm. **Fl**: Jan–Apr. **Distr**: N, E.

APOCYNACEAE

Subfamily Periplocoideae

Raphionacme hirsuta

Erect, branched herb with stems from large, flattened, circular, perennial underground tuber. Leaves few, short-stalked, broadly ovate, hairy, midrib conspicuous. Flowers star-shaped, bright magenta, purple or deep pink, hairy.

Ht: up to 30 cm. **Fl**: Oct–Nov. **Distr**: T.

Subfamily Asclepiadoideae

Xysmalobium asperum

Small, erect herb usually with single stem from tuberous rootstock. Leaves opposite, ovate, conspicuously veined. Flowers small, brownish purple, in a terminal, many-flowered umbel.

Ht: up to 30 cm. **Fl**: Oct–Dec. **Distr**: T.

Asclepias dissona

Low herb with several slender, smooth stems from tuberous rootstock. Leaves opposite, linear-lanceolate, lobed at base. Flowers purplish, in a terminal, 5-flowered umbel.

Ht: up to 20 cm. **Fl:** Oct–Dec. **Distr:** N, E.

Ceropegia crassifolia var. *crassifolia*

Twiner with annual, succulent, smooth, unbranched stems from perennial rootstock with a cluster of long, fleshy roots. Leaves fleshy, linear, with crisped margin. Flowers tubular, inflated at base, pale green with purple markings.

Fl: Jan–Mar. **Distr:** T.

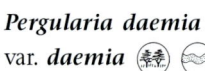

Pergularia daemia var. *daemia*

Herbaceous twiner with milky sap, hairy throughout. Leaves heart-shaped, opposite. Flowers small, varying from white to green or yellow, sometimes tinged with purple, bell-shaped, opening towards evening.

Ht: up to 1 m. **Fl:** Oct–Dec. **Distr:** N, W, E.

CONVOLVULACEAE

Ipomoea bathycolpos

Perennial with several annual, roughly hairy, prostrate stems from woody taproot. Leaves heart-shaped, with deep basal sinus, margins thickened, shallowly toothed. Flowers funnel-shaped, pale mauve to almost white with darker mauve-magenta margins.

Fl: Oct–Mar. **Distr:** T.

Ipomoea crassipes

One-day Flower; Wildepatatta, Wildewinde

Perennial herb with hairy, prostrate, trailing, purplish stems from large underground rhizome. Leaves ovate, hairy, with purplish margin. Flowers solitary, axillary, funnel-shaped, magenta or pink, soon withering.

Fl: Sep–Jan. **Distr**: T.

Ipomoea ommaneyi

Robust, perennial herb, densely woolly throughout with long, trailing stems from thick, tuberous rootstock. Leaves long-stalked, broadly ovate, with wavy, yellow margins. Flowers axillary, funnel-shaped, pale purple to rose-magenta.

Fl: Oct–Mar. **Distr**: T.

Ipomoea papilio

Perennial with slender, hairy, trailing or climbing stems. Leaves triangular, deeply toothed towards base, with broad basal sinus. Flowers funnel-shaped, light magenta or rose-red, in 1- or 2–5-flowered, axillary cymes.

Fl: Sep–May. **Distr**: T.

VERBENACEAE

Lantana rugosa

Bird's Brandy; Voëlbrandewyn

Small, much-branched, aromatic shrub. Leaves opposite or in whorls of 3 or 4, prominently veined on lower surface, margin deeply toothed. Flowers pink, orange, purple or magenta. Fruit globose, fleshy, purple drupes.

Ht: up to 60 cm. **Fl**: Oct–Mar. **Distr**: T.

Verbena bonariensis

Purple Top, Wild Verbena; Blou-waterbossie, Wildeverbena

Tall, robust, erect, much-branched herb with 4-angled stems, shortly hairy. Flowers purple, in terminal, congested, long-stalked inflorescences.

Ht: up to 2 m. **Fl**: Oct–Apr. **Distr**: T.

Verbena tenuisecta

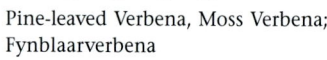

Pine-leaved Verbena, Moss Verbena; Fynblaarverbena

Prostrate to suberect, perennial herb with slender, 4-angled, hairy stems from woody rootstock. Leaves opposite, deeply once or twice divided. Flowers tubular, bright mauve fading blue, in dense, terminal clusters.

Ht: up to 60 cm. **Fl**: Oct–Feb. **Distr**: T.

Verbena venosa
Vervain

Erect, branched, rather stiff, often low-growing herb. Leaves sharply toothed, prominently veined. Flowers tubular, bright magenta-purple, in terminal, congested heads.

Ht: up to 75 cm. **Fl**: Nov–Mar. **Distr**: T.

Chascanum latifolium var. ***latifolium***

Erect herb, much-branched, forming small bushes. Leaves fleshy, broadest towards tip, tapering to base, toothless. Flowers shortly stalked, tubular, with broad, blunt lobes, white or pale mauve.

Ht: up to 50 cm. **Fl**: Sep–Nov. **Distr**: S, E.

LAMIACEAE

Ajuga ophrydis

Decumbent, perennial herb with white-woolly stems, much-branched from short rhizome. Leaves sessile, mainly in basal rosette, thick, hairy, margins toothed. Flowers tubular, blue, lilac to mauve, rarely white, in well-spaced, crowded rows.

Ht: up to 25 cm. **Fl**: Sep–Jan. **Distr**: E, S.

Scutellaria racemosa
Skullcap

Weak-stemmed, perennial herb with much-branched, sparsely hairy stems. Leaves stalked, gland-dotted below, with entire margins. Flowers tubular, violet to red or white with purple spots, in lax, axillary clusters.

Ht: up to 30 cm. **Fl**: Oct–Jan. **Distr**: C.

Mentha longifolia subsp. *polyadena*

Spreading, perennial, aromatic herb, almost hairless, gland-dotted. Leaves almost sessile, narrowly lance-shaped, smooth on both surfaces. Inflorescence cylindrical, dense, many-flowered. Flowers pale mauve or whitish.

Ht: up to 1.5 m. **Fl**: Dec–Mar. **Distr**: T.

Endostemon tereticaulis

Perennial, dwarf, aromatic shrublet with closely leafy, branched, hairy stems. Leaves subsessile, hairy on both surfaces. Inflorescence in 6-flowered rows. Flowers tubular, mauve to purple; calyx with winged lateral teeth.

Ht: up to 50 cm. **Fl**: Oct–Mar.
Distr: N, W, E.

Plectranthus neochilus
Lobster Flower

Decumbent to erect, perennial, strong-smelling herb with glandular-hairy stems, sticky to the touch. Leaves simple, fleshy, ovate, shallowly toothed. Flowers tubular, pale mauve, in terminal, well-spaced inflorescences.

Ht: up to 50 cm. **Fl**: Sep–Apr.
Distr: N, E, W, C.

Hemizygia foliosa

Perennial herb with several semi-erect, hairy stems from woody rootstock. Leaves subsessile, hairy, gland-dotted on both surfaces. Flowers tubular, white to mauve; stamens exserted.

Ht: up to 40 cm. **Fl**: Sep–Nov, sometimes later. **Distr**: S, E.

Becium obovatum subsp. *obovatum* var. *obovatum*
Cat's Whiskers, I Spy

Perennial herb with erect, thinly hairy stems from woody rootstock. Leaves subsessile, opposite, hairy, margins toothed or entire. Inflorescence with 1–3 well-spaced rows of flowers. Flowers white to pale mauve; stamens exserted.

Ht: up to 30 cm. **Fl**: Sep–Feb. **Distr**: T.

SOLANACEAE

Solanum panduriforme

Apple of Sodom, Poison Apple, Bitter Apple; Geelappel, Bitterappel, Gifappel

Similar to *S. tomentosum coccineum* (p. 52) but differs in having purple flowers, larger, yellow fruits and entire to shallowly lobed leaves.

Ht: up to 40 cm. **Fl**: Nov–Feb. **Distr**: T.

Solanum sisymbriifolium

Dense-thorned Bitter Apple, Wild Tomato; Digdoringbitterappel, Doringtamatie

Erect, much-branched shrub, densely spiny with strong, orange-red spines. Leaves deeply divided; lobes further lobed, toothed, hairy on both surfaces. Flowers white, cream-coloured, purple or bluish, hairy outside. Fruit a bright red, shiny berry.

Ht: up to 1.5 m. **Fl**: Nov–May. **Distr**: T.

SCROPHULARIACEAE

Aptosimum elongatum

Carpet Flower, Wild Violet, Violet-of-the-Karoo; Brandblare

Prostrate herb with long, trailing, much-branched, closely leafy stems from woody rootstock. Flowers tubular, axillary, dark blue to purple, sometimes with white mark on opposite side of lobes.

Fl: Dec–Apr. **Distr**: N, W, C, S.

Jamesbrittenia aurantiaca
Cape Saffron; Saffraanbossie

Small, slender, erect, aromatic herb from perennial rootstock. Leaves deeply divided; lobes further divided. Flowers small, tubular, orange-red, pink or purple with darker centre.

Ht: up to 20 cm. **Fl**: Oct–Mar. **Distr**: T.

Jamesbrittenia grandiflora

Robust erect undershrub, shortly hairy, glandular throughout. Leaves irregularly short-toothed. Flowers mostly solitary or a few together, terminal, tubular, purple, mauve or violet; lobes gland-dotted.

Ht: up to 80 cm. **Fl**: Jan–Jul.
Distr: N, C, E.

Sutera caerulea
Ruikbossie

Robust, erect, much-branched, aromatic herb with shortly hairy stems. Leaves narrow, shallowly toothed towards tip. Flowers in dense, terminal clusters, purple, pale blue or pink, yellow inside.

Ht: up to 60 cm. **Fl**: Dec–Apr.
Distr: T.

Sutera neglecta

Robust, erect, much-branched herb from woody base. Leaves shallowly toothed. Flowers tubular, sweetly scented, deep mauve, violet or pink, in terminal clusters.

Ht: up to 30 cm. **Fl**: Dec–Mar. **Distr**: S, E.

Selago capitellata

Erect shrublet with closely leafy, much-branched, hairy stems. Leaves linear, needle-like, in whorls. Flowers small, tubular, white, lilac, or blue in terminal, clusters.

Ht: up to 30 cm. **Fl**: Oct–Mar. **Distr**: T.

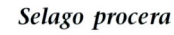

Selago procera

Robust, much-branched shrublet, thinly hairy. Leaves sessile, broadly lanceolate or ovate, well-spaced. Flowers tubular, white or pale mauve or pink, in small, loose, few-flowered, terminal heads.

Ht: up to 1 m. **Fl**: Sep–May. **Distr**: N, E.

Tetraselago wilmsii

Tufted, woody, perennial herb with closely leafy, straggling or prostrate stems. Leaves ovate, sharply acute, toothed. Flowers lilac, occasionally white or pale blue, in dense, terminal, dome-shaped heads.

Ht: up to 50 cm. **Fl**: Jan–Mar. **Distr**: N, E.

Veronica anagallis-aquatica

Water Speedwell; Ereprys, Waterereprys

Erect, annual herb, often rooting at lower nodes, with smooth, fleshy stems. Leaves sessile, opposite. Flowers small, pale blue to purple, in a dense, axillary raceme.

Ht: up to 60 cm. **Fl**: indefinite. **Distr**: T.

Striga bilabiata

Tall, erect, hemiparasitic herb with slender stems, turning black when dried. Leaves linear, opposite, coarsely hairy, pressed up against the stem. Flowers white to lilac, tubular.

Ht: up to 20 cm. **Fl**: Oct–Feb, sometimes May–Jun. **Distr**: T.

Striga gesnerioides

Purple Witchweed, Tobacco Witchweed; Bloublom, Rooiblommetjie

Dwarf hemiparasite, branched from base, drying black. Leaves simple, linear, pressed up against the stem. Flowers tubular, deep purple, in terminal spike.

Ht: up to 15 cm. **Fl:** Jan–Apr. **Distr:** T.

PEDALIACEAE
Pterodiscus speciosus

Small, erect, perennial herb with slender stems from woody rootstock. Leaves linear-lanceolate, opposite or sub-opposite, sharply toothed. Flowers funnel-shaped, red and purple, axillary. Fruit ovate, winged, brown.

Ht: up to 20 cm. **Fl:** Oct–Jan. **Distr:** T.

Ceratotheca triloba

Rhodesian Foxglove, Wild Foxglove; Vingerhoedblom, Vingerhoedbossie

Tall, slender, erect, annual herb with hairy stems. Leaves opposite, deeply 3-lobed, strong-smelling when crushed, margins bluntly toothed. Flowers solitary, axillary, funnel-shaped, pale pink, pinkish mauve or white.

Ht: up to 2 m. **Fl:** Dec–Feb. **Distr:** N, W, C, E.

ACANTHACEAE
Barleria meyeriana

Slender, erect, elongated, irregularly branched, subwoody herb. Leaves unequal-sided at base. Flowers solitary, axillary, tubular with spreading lobes, pale blue or mauve.

Ht: up to 50 cm. **Fl:** Feb–Apr. **Distr:** E.

Barleria pretoriensis

Small, perennial herb or low shrub with branched, hairy, decumbent, woody stems from woody rootstock. Leaves ovate, tapering to both ends. Flowers tubular, 5-lobed, solitary, cream-coloured in bud, opening white, turning mauve with age.

Ht: up to 60 cm. **Fl**: Feb–Apr. **Distr**: N, W, C.

Sclerochiton harveyanus

Erect, irregularly branched shrub or scrambler with thinly shortly hairy branches. Leaves opposite, dark green above, paler below, with shallowly toothed margins. Flowers with corolla limb split open with 5-lobed lip on one side, purple.

Ht: up to 3 m. **Fl**: Dec–Mar. **Distr**: N, E.

Dicliptera clinopodia

Erect or straggling undershrub, thinly hairy throughout. Leaves ovate, narrowing to tip, broad towards base. Inflorescences dense, shortly stalked clusters, in well-spaced rows. Bracts narrow, finely pointed. Flowers tubular, magenta, violet or purple.

Ht: up to 1 m. **Fl**: Mar–Aug. **Distr**: N, E.

Siphonoglossa linifolia
(= *Aulojusticia*)

Slender, erect herb or shrublet, much-branched from woody base. Leaves simple, opposite, linear-lanceolate, sessile. Flowers long, tubular, axillary, hairy, 2-lipped, lower lip 3-lobed, mauve with darker spots on lower lip.

Ht: up to 30 cm. **Fl**: Feb–Mar. **Distr**: E.

RUBIACEAE

Kohautia virgata

Slender, erect, much-branched herb. Leaves narrow, in well-spaced whorls. Flowers tubular, mauve to red to white with pale mauve stripe on outside.

Ht: up to 30 cm. **Fl**: Sep–Dec. **Distr**: T.

Conostomium natalense var. ***glabrum***

Robust, erect, perennial herb with several reddish stems from woody rootstock. Leaves opposite, decreasing in size upwards. Flowers tubular, lilac to pale blue, in terminal, axillary clusters.

Ht: up to 30 cm. **Fl**: Nov–Mar. **Distr**: N, E.

CAMPANULACEAE

Wahlenbergia denticulata
(= *Lightfootia denticulata*)

Slender, erect, annual herb, much-branched in upper half. Leaves small, linear, alternate, toothed. Flowers small, deeply lobed, star-shaped, shortly stalked, terminal, violet, mauve or blue.

Ht: up to 30 cm. **Fl**: Aug–Mar. **Distr**: T.

Wahlenbergia krebsii subsp. *krebsii*

Perennial, erect, sometimes procumbent herb from taproot. Leaves alternate, sessile, crowded towards base, margins wavy, toothed. Flowers subsessile, white to blue or violet, often with dark veins, in lax inflorescences.

Ht: up to 50 cm. **Fl:** Dec–Mar. **Distr:** N, C, E, S.

ASTERACEAE
Bothriocline laxa

Erect, annual, leafy herb, hairy throughout. Florets pale mauve, in small, loosely branched, flat-topped flowerheads.

Ht: up to 80 cm. **Fl:** Feb–Jun, sometimes later. **Distr:** N, E.

Vernonia fastigiata
Bloutee(bossie), Langbeenbossie

Low, much-branched, bushy herb, slightly woody, thinly downy throughout. Florets bright purple or magenta on slender-stalked, globose flowerheads.

Ht: up to 50 cm. **Fl:** Jul–Jan, sometimes later. **Distr:** T.

Vernonia galpinii

Slender, erect, leafy, annual herb with hairy stems from perennial rootstock. Leaves sessile. Florets purple. Flowerheads terminal, solitary or sometimes 3 or 4 together.

Ht: up to 30 cm. **Fl:** Aug–Feb. **Distr:** T.

Vernonia myriantha
Blue Bitter Tea, Poison Tree Vernonia;
Bloubittertee, Bosbloutee

Erect shrub, usually branched at base.
Leaves large, undersurface downy,
upper surface thinly hairy, darker.
Florets pale mauve, in many flowerheads
arranged in a rather loose dome-shaped
inflorescence.

Ht: up to 3 m. **Fl**: May–Jul. **Distr**: N, E.

Vernonia natalensis

Erect herb with closely leafy, annual
stems from woody rootstock. Leaves
sessile, silvery hairy. Florets purple, in
discoid flowerheads at ends of branches.

Ht: up to 60 cm. **Fl**: Jul–Dec. **Distr**: T.

Vernonia oligocephala
Amarabossie

Slender, erect, closely leafy, annual herb from
perennial rootstock. Leaves ovate, silvery hairy
on lower surface. Florets few, purple, in small,
compact, terminal capitula.

Ht: up to 60 cm. **Fl**: Aug–Jan. **Distr**: T.

Vernonia poskeana
subsp. ***botswanica***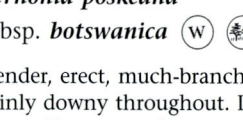

Slender, erect, much-branched herb,
thinly downy throughout. Leaves sessile,
linear. Florets purple, mauve or magenta,
in terminal, stalked flowerheads.

Ht: up to 60 cm. **Fl**: Mar–Jun. **Distr**: T.

Vernonia staehelinoides
Bloutee(bossie)

Tall, slender, erect, perennial herb, much-branched. Leaves grey-green above, white-woolly below, margins inrolled. Florets deep purple, in terminal, elongated capitula.

Ht: up to 60 cm. **Fl**: Mar–May. **Distr**: T.

Vernonia sutherlandii

Erect, much-branched, perennial herb with densely hairy stems from woody rootstock. Leaves sessile, sharply toothed, hairy. Florets deep purple or magenta, in few flowerheads at end of common stalk.

Ht: up to 60 cm. **Fl**: Sep–Feb (flowering out of season after unusual rain or veld fire). **Distr**: T.

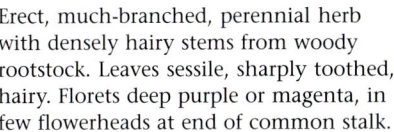

Aster harveyanus

Slender, erect, perennial herb. Leaves simple, alternate, irregularly toothed. Flowerheads solitary, terminal, long-stalked. Florets mauve, lilac or sometimes white.

Ht: up to 60 cm. **Fl**: Aug–Jan. **Distr**: T.

Felicia filifolia subsp. *filifolia*
Wild Aster

Much-branched shrublet, closely leafy. Leaves needle-like. Ray-florets mauve; disc-florets yellow, in capitula at ends of branches.

Ht: up to 60 cm. **Fl**: Jul–Mar. **Distr**: E, C, S.

Pseudoconyza viscosa
(= *Blumea aurita*)

Robust, erect, much-branched, closely leafy, annual herb with pungent odour. Leaves deeply cut towards centre; lobes sharply toothed. Flowerheads many, in branched clusters at ends of branchlets. Florets purple.

Ht: up to 50 cm. **Fl**: May–Oct. **Distr**: N, E.

Litogyne gariepina
(= *Epaltes gariepina*)
Blougifbossie

Small, closely leafy, much-branched, bushy, perennial herb. Leaves sessile, lanceolate, faintly toothed. Flowerheads in compact, terminal clusters. Florets magenta, mauve or pink.

Ht: up to 30 cm. **Fl**: Sep–Nov, sometimes later. **Distr**: T.

Athrixia phylicoides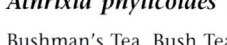
Bushman's Tea, Bush Tea; Beesbossie, Boesmanstee

Robust, much branched, leafy shrub. Leaves linear, smooth above, white-felted below. Ray-florets mauve; disc-florets yellow, in sessile, terminal and axillary flowerheads.

Ht: up to 1 m. **Fl**: throughout the year. **Distr**: N, E, S.

Lopholaena coriifolia
Geelbossie; Pluisbossie

Small, erect, much-branched shrub. Leaves strap-shaped, stem-clasping, grey-waxy. Florets pale yellow or mauve, in shortly stalked flowerheads, solitary or few together.

Ht: up to 50 cm. **Fl**: Oct–Nov. **Distr**: T.

Crassocephalum crepidioides

Slender, erect, annual herb, thinly downy, with ribbed stems. Leaves deeply divided; lobes irregularly toothed. Inflorescence terminal, loosely branched. Florets pink, mauve or purple, in long-stalked flowerheads.

Ht: up to 75 cm. **Fl**: Feb–May. **Distr**: N, E.

Senecio erubescens var. *crepidifolius*

Perennial herb with densely leafy, glandular-hairy flowering-stems, solitary, decumbent, becoming erect. Flowerheads racemosely arranged, differing from those of var. *dichotomus* which are corymbose-paniculately arranged. Florets deep purple.

Ht: up to 70 cm. **Fl**: Sep–Dec.
Distr: N, W, S, E.

Senecio polyodon var. *subglaber*

Tall, slender, erect, perennial herb. Basal leaves in rosettes. Flowerheads rayed, magenta-pink, purple or blue, few to many, in terminal inflorescences.

Ht: up to 75 cm. **Fl**: Oct–Jan. **Distr**: E, S.

Senecio speciosus
American Groundsel

Robust, erect herb with many flowering-stems from thick, woody rootstock. Leaves in basal rosette, white-woolly below. Flowerheads terminal, in small groups. Ray-florets pink to purple.

Ht: up to 60 cm. **Fl**: Jul–Jan, or indefinite. **Distr**: E.

Emilia transvaalensis

Bushy, annual herb with woody, leafy stems. Leaves crowded, slightly fleshy, stem-clasping. Flowers lilac, in solitary, long-stalked, discoid heads.

Ht: up to 45 cm. **Fl**: throughout the year. **Distr**: N, C, W, E.

Dimorphotheca jucunda
Bergbietou, Bloutou

Slender, perennial herb with erect, thinly downy stems from slender rootstock. Flowerheads solitary, on long, slender stalks. Ray-florets magenta; disc-florets yellow.

Ht: up to 45 cm. **Fl**: Sep–Apr. **Distr**: N, W, E, S.

Dimorphotheca spectabilis
Bietou, Bloutou

Robust, erect, perennial herb with stout, simple flowering-stems from woody rootstock. Flowerheads showy, solitary. Ray-florets blue or purple, surrounding the violet disc-florets.

Ht: up to 60 cm. **Fl**: Sep–Dec. **Distr**: W, C, E, S.

Cirsium vulgare
Scotch Thistle, Spear Thistle; Disseldoring, Skotse Dissel

Robust, erect, biennial herb with leafy, sparsely hairy stems. Leaves deeply lobed; lobes ending in strong spines, white-felted on lower surface, margins with smaller spines. Flowerheads subsessile at ends of branches. Florets mauve. Involucral bracts in many rows, spiny.

Ht: up to 90 cm. **Fl**: Jan–Jul. **Distr**: T.

Dicoma anomala
Aambeibos, Gryshout, Kalwerbossie, Maagbitterwortel

Erect, perennial herb with few to many stiff, ribbed stems from stout rootstock. Leaves narrow, smooth, dark green above, white-felted below. Flowerheads solitary, terminal. Involucral bracts erect, in rows, pointed. Florets purplish or white.

Ht: up to 30 cm. **Fl**: Feb–May. **Distr**: T.

Dicoma anomala

Different prostrate form. Flowerheads solitary or few at branch tips.

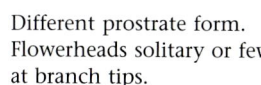

Dicoma zeyheri subsp. *zeyheri*
Toy Sugarbush, Doll's Protea; Jakkalsbos

Robust, erect, perennial herb from stout, woody rootstock. Leaves smooth above, white-felted below. Flowerheads solitary or few, terminal. Involucral bracts in many rows, narrow, sharply pointed. Florets white with purple or green tinge.

Ht: up to 40 cm. **Fl**: Feb–May **Distr**: T.

Red Flowers

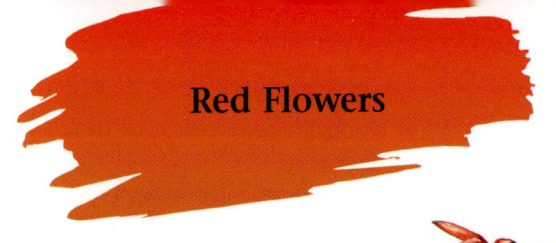

ASPHODELACEAE

Aloe arborescens

Robust, much-branched shrub. Branches ending in large rosettes of many leaves. Leaves recurved, tapering from base to apex, without spots, margins with broad, blunt teeth. Inflorescence simple or branched. Flowers tubular, vermilion.

Ht: 2–3 m. **Fl**: Apr–Jul. **Distr**: N, E.

Aloe branddraaiensis

Plants solitary or in groups of 5 or 6. Leaves in a basal rosette, 20–25, upper surface green at base, brownish towards tip, with striations and irregularly scattered 'H' spots, margins with sharp, pale brown teeth. Inflorescence much-branched from middle. Flowers tubular, scarlet-red.

Ht: up to 1.5 m. **Fl**: Jun–Jul. **Distr**: E.

Aloe verecunda

Robust, erect plant, solitary or in groups. Leaves succulent, fleshy, up to 12, lower surface with small, white spots near base, margins with small, soft, white teeth. Inflorescence simple, 20-flowered. Flowers tubular, pendulous, peach-red.

Ht: up to 40 cm. **Fl**: Nov–Mar. **Distr**: T.

AMARYLLIDACEAE

Scadoxus puniceus
Royal Paintbrush; Mieliegifbol

Robust, bulbous, perennial herb with large bulb covered with fleshy tunics. Leaves glossy, erect, stem-clasping, with tubular bases forming pseudostems. Inflorescence a dense, many-flowered umbel; stalk compressed, spotted with purple. Involucral bracts deep red. Flowers tubular, orange-red, with many exserted stamens. Fruit fleshy, globose, scarlet.

Ht: up to 40 cm. **Fl**: Sep–Nov. **Distr**: T.

Cyrtanthus bicolor

Slender, bulbous plant with ovoid bulb contracted into neck, with 1 or 2 brown tunics. Leaves linear, appearing after flowers. Flowers nodding, narrowly funnel-shaped, red or yellow, in 3–10-flowered umbels.

Ht: up to 30 cm. **Fl**: throughout the year. **Distr**: E.

Cyrtanthus contractus
Fire Lily; Brandlelie

Perennial herb with ovoid bulb covered with brown tunic. Leaves 2 or 3, basal, linear. Flowering-stem purplish. Inflorescence 4–10-flowered. Flowers pendulous, tubular, scarlet to carmine.

Ht: up to 30 cm. **Fl**: Aug–Nov. **Distr**: E, S.

IRIDACEAE

Hesperantha coccinea
(= *Schizostylis coccinea*)
Crimson Flag, Flame Lily

Perennial herb growing in clumps, with a matted rootstock. Leaves few, linear, basal. Flowers showy, scarlet with satin sheen, 4–10 on a slender stalk, each with 2 green bracts.

Ht: up to 70 cm. **Fl**: Dec–Mar. **Distr**: N, C, E, S.

Crocosmia paniculata

Robust, erect, smooth, herbaceous perennial with slender flowering-stems from corm covered with fibrous tunics. Leaves linear, fluted. Inflorescence stout, rigid, zigzagging. Flowers tubular, widening at mouth, yellow or orange, curving slightly.

Ht: 1–1.3 m. **Fl**: Dec–Feb. **Distr**: E, S.

Gladiolus dalenii

Robust, erect perennial with globose corm covered with soft brown fibres. Leaves 5–12, in a fan. Flowers funnel-shaped, recurved, streaked and mottled in combinations of green, brown, orange, yellow and red, or plain orange-red or yellow.

Ht: up to 60 cm. **Fl**: Sep–May. **Distr**: T.

Freesia grandiflora
(= *Anomatheca grandiflora*)

Small, erect herb with flowering-stem from small, globose corm covered with an outer matted brown tunic. Leaves slender, linear, flat, in 2 rows. Flowers tubular, scarlet, in lax spike. Fruit a capsule with few shiny red seeds.

Ht: up to 50 cm. **Fl**: Oct–Jan. **Distr**: T.

LORANTHACEAE

Tapinanthus rubromarginatus

Relatively large, parasitic shrubs on trees. Stems thick, with scattered lenticels. Leaves in crowded fascicles, deciduous, elliptic, with red margins. Inflorescences 2–4-flowered umbels. Flowers tubular with large basal swelling, dark red to purplish with darker lobes, sometimes with scattered white spots.

Ht: up to 1 m. **Fl**: Sep–Nov. **Distr**: T.

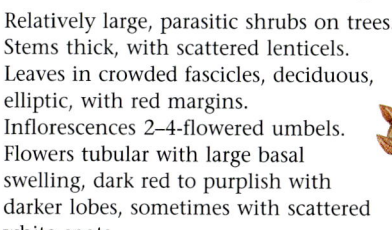

POLYGONACEAE

Rumex acetosella subsp. *angiocarpus*

Sheep Sorrel; Steenboksuring

Slender, erect, annual herb, much-branched from base. Leaves arrowhead-shaped, long-stalked. Flowers small, cup-shaped, rose-red, in many terminal clusters; stamens bright yellow.

Ht: up to 1 m. **Fl**: Sep–Mar. **Distr**: T.

PORTULACACEAE

Portulaca quadrifida

Pusley, Wild Purslane; Kanniedood, Porselein

Prostrate, annual herb, much-branched, long-silky hairy at nodes. Leaves succulent. Flowers terminal, solitary, yellow, pink, purple, magenta-red or scarlet.

Ht: up to 10 cm. **Fl**: Dec–May. **Distr**: T.

CRASSULACEAE

Kalanchoe rotundifolia

Nenta Kalanchoe; Nentabos, Plakkie

Erect, sparsely branched, succulent shrublet. Leaves fleshy, shortly stalked or sessile, opposite, blue-green, margins entire, dentate or lobed. Inflorescence a sparsely flowered thyrse. Flowers tubular, orange to deep red.

Ht: up to 1.2 m. **Fl**: Mar–Aug. **Distr**: T.

Crassula alba var. *alba*

Perennial or biennial herb with erect reddish, fleshy stems. Leaves lance-shaped, in pairs spirally arranged. Inflorescence a flat-topped thyrse. Flowers tubular, deep red, pink or white.

Ht: up to 50 cm. **Fl**: Feb–Apr.
Distr: N, C, E, S.

FABACEAE

Trifolium africanum var. *africanum*

African Wild Clover, Wild Clover; Afrikaanse Klawer, Wildeklawer

Low-growing, prostrate, perennial herb with smooth to sparsely hairy stems. Leaves 3-foliolate; leaflets 2–4 times longer than broad, margin finely serrate. Flowers red to purple, in long-stalked, globose heads.

Fl: Nov–Apr. **Distr**: T.

Indigofera daleoides
var. *daleoides*

Erect to decumbent herb with densely hairy, much-branched stems from woody rootstock. Leaves compound, with more than 8 alternate, densely hairy leaflets. Flowers small, red or pink, in dense, axillary, long-stalked clusters, interspersed with long, linear bracts.

Ht: up to 30 cm. **Fl**: Sep–Feb. **Distr**: T.

Indigofera melanadenia

Erect, straggling, woody shrublet. Leaves compound, with 6–9 opposite leaflets; leaflets silvery silky hairy, with dark spot at base. Flowers small, red, in dense, axillary, terminal, long-stalked inflorescences.

Ht: up to 1 m. **Fl**: Dec–Feb. **Distr**: T.

Indigofera oxytropis

Sprawling, perennial herb with velvety hairy stems from woody rootstock. Leaves compound, with 7 pairs of opposite leaflets and a terminal one; leaflets hairy on undersurface. Flowers deep red.

Ht: up to 30 cm. **Fl**: Oct–Feb. **Distr**: W, C, S.

Indigofera setiflora

Robust, erect herb, much-branched from woody rootstock. Leaves compound, with 5–9 linear to ovate, well-spaced leaflets, hairy on upper surface. Flowers small, deep pink to red, in long-stalked axillary raceme. Fruit globose, hairy.

Ht: up to 50 cm.
Fl: Nov–Feb. **Distr**: T.

Erythrina zeyheri

Plough-breaker; Ploegbreker

Robust, erect herb with annual, prickly shoots from large, tuberous rootstock. Leaves 3-foliolate; leaflets large, with scattered recurved prickles. Flowers bright scarlet, in triangular flowerheads.

Ht: up to 30 cm. **Fl**: Oct–Jan.
Distr: W, C, E, S.

Dolichos angustifolius

Erect herb with slender stems from woody rootstock. Leaves compound, with linear leaflets. Flowers rose-red to pink, few, in axillary clusters.

Ht: up to 30 cm. **Fl**: Aug–Dec.
Distr: W, C, E, S.

EUPHORBIACEAE

Acalypha peduncularis

Brooms and Brushes, Wild Acalypha

Slender, semi-erect, perennial herb with stems from woody rootstock, densely hairy throughout. Leaves alternate, sessile, broadly ovate, conspicuously veined, sharply toothed. Male and female flowers on separate plants; males red with cream-coloured anthers, in long-stalked, elongated, axillary inflorescences; females red, terminal.

Ht: up to 30 cm. **Fl**: Sep–Jan. **Distr**: T.

STERCULIACEAE

Hermannia depressa

Rooi-opslag

Prostrate herb with spreading, sparsely hairy and glandular stems from woody rootstock. Leaves ovate, bluntly toothed. Flowers orange-yellow with pink or reddish flush, few, in terminal inflorescences.

Fl: Oct–Jan. **Distr**: T.

GUNERACEAE

Gunnera perpensa

River Pumpkin; Rivierpampoen

Perennial herb without aerial stems. Leaves large, from rhizome, heart-shaped at base. Inflorescence also arising from ground. Flowers small, reddish, uni- or bisexual.

Ht: up to 60 cm. **Fl**: Nov–Jan. **Distr**: T.

SCROPHULARIACEAE

Striga asiatica

Common Mealie-witchweed; Gewone-mielierooiblom

Small, slender, erect, annual herb. Leaves alternate, linear-lanceolate. Flowers small, tubular, scarlet inside, orange outside.

Ht: up to 15 cm. **Fl**: Nov–Mar. **Distr**: C, E, S.

Striga elegans

Large Mealie-witchweed, Witchweed; Groot-mielierooiblom, Kopseerblommetjie

Small, slender, erect, parasitic herb. Leaves linear, opposite. Flowers terminal, showy, tubular, bright scarlet inside, apricot-yellow outside.

Ht: up to 20 cm. **Fl**: Dec–Mar. **Distr**: T.

ACANTHACEAE

Crossandra greenstockii
Rooiblom

Low, erect herb with long flowering-stem from clustered basal leaves and woody rootstock. Leaves ovate, blunt, hairy. Inflorescence unbranched, with broad, overlapping, hairy bracts. Flowers tubular, scarlet, orange or yellow, carried beyond bracts.

Ht: up to 30 cm. **Fl**: Oct–Mar. **Distr**: N, W, C, E.

ASTERACEAE

Zinnia peruviana

Redstar Zinnia; Wildejakobregop

Erect, annual herb with simple or branched stems, sparsely hairy. Leaves opposite, usually 3-veined. Flowerheads terminal, solitary. Ray-florets brick-red or purple.

Ht: up to 60 cm. **Fl**: Oct–Feb, sometimes later. **Distr**: T.

Crassocephalum crepidioides

Red flower colour form (see p. 183).

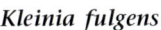

Kleinia fulgens
(= *Notoniopsis fulgens*)

Perennial herb with erect or decumbent, succulent stems. Leaves succulent, narrowing to a winged base. Flowerheads few, globose, scarlet, crimson or cerise.

Ht: up to 60 cm. **Fl**: May–Jul. **Distr**: N, C, W, E.

Gerbera jamesonii

Barberton Daisy; Rooigousblom

Erect, perennial herb. Leaves basal, long-stalked, deeply lobed and toothed, stalk reddish towards base. Flowering-head solitary, long-stalked. Ray-florets many, narrow, cream-coloured, red, scarlet, pink or pinkish yellow. Disc-florets yellow.

Ht: up to 50 cm. **Fl**: Aug–Nov. **Distr**: N, E, S.

Brown Flowers

HYACINTHACEAE

Urginea multisetosa

Slender, erect flowering-stem from large bulb with fibrous crown of bristles formed from old leaf bases. Leaves 2, appearing after flowers, grass-like, slightly twisted. Flowers pinkish brown, with whitish margins.

Ht: up to 30 cm. **Fl**: Aug–Nov. **Distr**: T.

Dipcadi marlothii

Slender, erect geophyte with small, white, fleshy bulb. Leaves slender, basal, bristly at base. Flowers tubular, brownish.

Ht: up to 30 cm. **Fl**: Aug–Dec. **Distr**: T.

IRIDACEAE

Gladiolus woodii

Erect plant with slender flowering-stem from globose to ovoid corm covered with tunic of reddish brown, matted fibres. Basal leaf solitary, linear. Inflorescence a 4–12-flowered spike. Flowers small, tubular, 2-lipped, varying from pale blue to deep red.

Ht: up to 60 cm. **Fl**: Oct–Dec.
Distr: N, C, E, S.

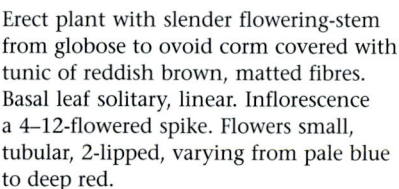

ORCHIDACEAE

Corycium nigrescens

Slender to robust, erect herb. Leaves lanceolate. Inflorescence a dense spike. Flowers purple-brown to almost black, with purplish green lip and lateral sepals joined for most of their length.

Ht: up to 40 cm. **Fl**: Dec–Feb. **Distr**: E.

APOCYNACEAE

Subfamily Asclepiadoideae
Xysmalobium parviflorum

Robust, erect, much-branched, perennial herb. Leaves rough, red-rimmed. Flowers strongly scented, white or greenish brown, with erect, red, pink or mauve, densely hairy calyx lobes.

Ht: up to 20 cm. **Fl**: Oct–Dec.
Distr: N, C, E, S.

Aspidoglossum lamellatum

Tall, slender, perennial herb with erect, hairy stems from woody rootstock. Leaves linear, opposite. Flowers small, brownish or dull yellow, a few together, axillary, shortly stalked. Fruit paired follicles curved upwards.

Ht: up to 50 cm. **Fl**: Oct–Dec.
Distr: W, C, E, S.

Miraglossum pilosum

Slender, erect herb with unbranched stem from tuberous rootstock, shortly hairy throughout. Leaves sessile, opposite. Flowers small, greenish brown, with erect, purplish black appendages.

Ht: up to 30 cm. **Fl**: Nov. **Distr**: E, S.

Miraglossum pulchellum

Erect, unbranched herb, with slightly hairy stems from globose, tuberous rootstock. Leaves subopposite, margins recurved. Flowers greenish yellow, with orange-brown appendages bent outwards.

Ht: up to 30 cm. **Fl**: Sep–Nov. **Distr**: N, E, S.

Asclepias brevipes
Bokhorinkie

Slender, erect, perennial herb with purplish tinged stems from woody rootstock. Inflorescence a few-flowered umbel of green, purple-brown tinted, star-shaped flowers.

Ht: up to 20 cm. **Fl**: Sep–Nov. **Distr**: T.

Asclepias monticola

Small, slender, prostrate herb with stems branching from tuberous rootstock. Leaves ovate, opposite, shortly stalked. Flowers greenish brown, in a terminal, few-flowered umbel.

Fl: Nov. **Distr**: E.

Pentarrhinum insipidum
Donkieperske, Opklim, Wildekomkommer

Slender, branched, thinly hairy twiner. Leaves simple, opposite, ovate, long-stalked. Flowers small, green or yellow, with upper petal tips tinged purple-brown, in lateral pseudo-umbels. Fruit large, ovoid, green, with many protuberances, splitting open to reveal many seeds crowned with silky hairs.

Fl: Feb–Apr. **Distr**: T.

Sisyranthus randii

Tall, slender, erect herb, branched from base. Leaves linear, opposite. Flowers pale brown or greenish, in axillary, long-stalked umbels.

Ht: up to 50 cm. **Fl**: Sep–Nov. **Distr**: N, C, E, S.

Orbeopsis melanantha

Similar to *O. lutea* (p. 123) in habit, but differing in the flowers being reddish brown and having broad lobes.

Ht: up to 10 cm. **Fl**: Nov–Mar. **Distr**: W, C.

SCROPHULARIACEAE
Jamesbrittenia accrescens

Robust, soft, perennial shrub, branching from base, glandular-hairy throughout. Leaves aromatic, opposite, toothed. Flowers tubular, brown with pale margin, drying black.

Ht: up to 50 cm. **Fl**: Jul–Feb. **Distr**: N, E.

Green Flowers

HYACINTHACEAE
Bowiea volubilis

Geophyte with large, globose, underground bulb. Leaves few, basal, filiform, soon falling off. Flowering-stem annual, leafless, scrambling, succulent, much-branched. Flowers small, green, long-stalked.

Fl: any season. **Distr**: T.

Albuca glauca

Bulbous plant with 1 or 2 flowering-stems from white, ovoid bulb with dark brown tunic, soon disintegrating. Leaves 2 or 3. Inflorescence a lax 9–20-flowered raceme. Bracts reddish. Flowers grey-green to greenish white with a dark green keel.

Ht: up to 40 cm. **Fl**: Aug–Nov. **Distr**: T.

Dipcadi gracillimum
Ouma-se-groottoon

Slender, erect geophyte with many linear leaves and flowering-stem from globose bulb. Flowers tubular with spreading lobes, green.

Ht: up to 45 cm. **Fl**: Oct–Dec. **Distr**: T.

Dipcadi viride
Gifbolletjie, Skaamblommetjie

Erect geophyte with slender flowering-stem from firm, white, fleshy, scaly bulb. Leaves basal, 1–4 per shoot, linear. Inflorescence a lax raceme. Flowers tubular, green to brownish green, with linear segments at apex.

Ht: up to 50 cm. **Fl**: Nov–Dec. **Distr**: T.

Eucomis autumnalis subsp. *clavata*

Robust, erect geophyte, solitary from large, ovoid bulb with hard, dark brown tunic of membranous leaf bases. Leaves linear, elliptic, margins wavy. Inflorescence a central simple 55–120-flowered raceme topped with crown of 15–30 leafy bracts. Flowers white, yellow or green.

Ht: up to 50 cm. **Fl**: Jan–Apr. **Distr**: T.

ORCHIDACEAE
Habenaria filicornis

Slender, erect herb. Leaves narrow, suberect. Flowers many, green, in lax inflorescences; lip with 3 equal, narrow lobes and slender spur.

Ht: up to 50 cm. **Fl**: Jan–Mar. **Distr**: S, E.

Harbenaria nyikana

Robust, erect, unbranched herb. Leaves linear. Flowers many, green with paler centre; lip with 3 subequal lobes, spur swollen in upper half.

Ht: up to 50 cm. **Fl**: Mar–Apr. **Distr**: E.

Bonatea speciosa var. *antennifera*

Robust, erect, leafy ground orchid with flowering-stem from flattened tuber. Leaves dark green, broadly ovate. Inflorescence dense. Flowers green and white, with lower petal lobe narrowly linear.

Ht: up to 90 cm. **Fl**: Mar–Apr. **Distr**: W, C.

Eulophia foliosa

Stout, erect plant with flowering-stem from moniliform rhizome. Leaves stiffly erect. Flowers 6–40, in a dense mass, lime-green, lip ends tinged dark purple, pale purple or white.

Ht: up to 45 cm. **Fl**: Oct–Jan. **Distr**: N, E.

VISCACEAE

Viscum combreticola

Leafless, dioecious shrub, an aerial hemiparasite. Young branches yellowish green, strongly flattened, ribbed; older branches rounded. Male flowers solitary in axillary leaf scales; female flowers solitary in bracteal cups. Fruit an ellipsoid berry, orange when ripe.

Ht: up to 1 m. **Fl**: Feb–May. **Distr**: T.

Viscum rotundifolium

Mistletoe; Voëlent

Slender, much-branched parasite. Leaves small, opposite, almost circular in outline. Flowers small, green, in axillary clusters. Fruit a smooth, ovoid, red, orange or yellow berry.

Ht: up to 50 cm.
Fl: Oct–May. **Distr**: T.

PASSIFLORACEAE

Adenia glauca
Bobbejaangif

Climber, sometimes shrub-like; basal part a large, perennial, underground storage organ. Leaves 5-lobed to base, blue-green. Flowers tubiform, greenish, both male and female in axils of leaves.

Ht: up to 3.5 m. **Fl**: Aug–Jan.
Distr: W, C.

APOCYNACEAE

Subfamily Asclepiadoideae
Xysmalobium undulatum
Bitterhout, Bitterwortel

Tall, robust, erect, perennial herb with hairy, leafy stems. Leaves large, broad at base narrowly tapering, velvety hairy. Inflorescence with lateral umbels. Flowers small, creamy green to yellow, fringed with white hairs.

Ht: up to 1.8 m. **Fl**: Oct–Jan. **Distr**: T.

Schizoglossum bidens subsp. ***productum***

Slender, erect, closely leafy herb with single, unbranched stem from tuberous rootstock, hairy throughout. Leaves in whorls, dark green above, paler below. Flowers small, greenish tinged purple, or mauve, in terminal, branched umbels.

Ht: up to 30 cm. **Fl**: Nov–Jan. **Distr**: N, E.

Schizoglossum cordifolium

Slender, erect, unbranched herb with shortly hairy stems from tuberous rootstock. Leaves opposite, well spaced, narrowly heart-shaped, tapering to tip. Flowers yellow or greenish brown, with white edges, in a terminal umbel.

Ht: up to 50 cm. **Fl**: Oct–Nov. **Distr**: N, E.

Asclepias albens

Robust, erect or prostrate herb, roughly hairy throughout. Leaves opposite, broadly ovate, conspicuously veined. Flowers green or yellow, in dense, rounded, terminal umbels.

Ht: up to 30 cm. **Fl**: Dec–Jan. **Distr**: W, C, E, S.

Asclepias eminens

Slender herb with prostrate shoots, usually much-branched at base. Leaf margins recurved. Inflorescence terminal, with up to 8 rather large, greenish flowers with white corona.

Fl: Nov–Dec. **Distr**: T.

Asclepias gibba var. *gibba*

Slender, erect to decumbent, perennial herb, thinly hairy, much-branched at base. Leaves blue-green, tapering to a sharp point. Inflorescence terminal, with up to 8 greenish or greyish mauve, fragrant flowers.

Ht: up to 50 cm. **Fl**: Oct–Nov.
Distr: W, C, E, S.

Brachystelma circinatum

Perennial herb with much-branched, densely hairy stem from depressed tuber, often with slightly concave central area. Leaves linear to ovate, flat or folded upwards, entire or wavy. Flowers from green to white to maroon, with corolla lobes fused at top.

Ht: up to 30 cm. **Fl**: Nov–Dec.
Distr: C, S, W.

Glossary

A

above: of the upper surface of a leaf.
absent: missing, not present.
achene: one-seeded, dry fruit that does not split.
acuminate: having a long, slender, sharp point.
acute: sharp-pointed.
aggregate fruit: a cluster of fruits formed from the free carpels of one flower.
alternate: placed singly at different levels on stem or axis.
annual: of one season's duration from seed to maturity and death.
anther: top part of a stamen producing pollen.
apex: tip, topmost part or terminal end.
aquatic: living in water.
aromatic: strongly smelling.
ascending: rising obliquely or curving upwards from near the base.
axil: the angle between a stem and a leaf or bract.
axillary: growing in an axil.

B

basal: at the base of an organ; rising from the ground.
beak: a prominent terminal projection on certain fruits, seeds and carpels.
below: of the lower surface of a leaf.
berry: a fleshy fruit containing two or more seeds.
biennial: taking more than one but less than two years to complete its life cycle.
bilabiate: two-lipped, as when two or three lobes of a corolla stand separate as an upper lip from the others forming lower lip.
bilobed: having two lobes.
bisexual: having both sexes present and functional in one flower.
bladder: modified insectivorous leaf used to capture insects in the Bladderwort Family.
bract: a much-reduced leaf, borne in the region of the flowering part of the shoot.
bulb: an underground storage organ with fleshy, scaly leaves on a shortened stem.
bulbous: having a structure resembling a bulb.

C

calyx: an outer envelope of a flower, consisting of the sepals.
capitate: headed; in heads; formed like a head.
capitulum: an inflorescence characteristic of Asteraceae, the

Daisy Family, in which few to very many florets are borne on a disc-like receptacle surrounded by involucral bracts. The florets are frequently, but not always, differentiated into outer, petaloid ray-florets and inner, tubular disc-florets.

capsule: dry fruit with two or more carpels splitting open when ripe.

cauline: placed on stem.

cilia: small hairs.

ciliate: fringed with marginal hairs.

cladodes: leaf-like organs of *Asparagus*.

clasping: partly or wholly surrounding stems.

claw: the narrow base of a petal, sepal or bract.

compound: in several parts, as a leaf divided into leaflets.

cordate: applied to the base of a leaf when it is ± deeply notched.

corm: an underground shoot, consisting of a swollen underground stem, ± covered by membranous scales.

corolla: the petals of a flower, free or united.

corona: a crown; in some flowers, an appendage between the corolla and stamens which may be petaloid or staminal in origin; in some members of the Asclepiadoideae the corona consists of one or two alternating rows different in size and shape.

crisped: curled.

cyathium: a type of inflorescence found in *Euphorbia*.

cyme: type of inflorescence in which the oldest flowers are at the top.

D

deciduous: with leaves falling at the end of one season of growth or life.

decumbent: reclining or lying on the ground with the end rising.

deltoid: shaped ± like an equal-sided triangle.

digitate: hand-like.

dioecious: unisexual, with the male and female flowers on different plants.

disc-florets: tubular florets usually found with ray-florets in Asteraceae (Daisy Family).

discoid: like a dish or plate.

dorsal: of a carpel or leaf, the back, or the face turned away from the axis.

E

elliptic: oval in outline.

elongated: stretched out, made longer.

entire: not divided, e.g. a leaf margin.

epiphyte: a plant growing on another, but receiving no nourishment from that plant.

exserted: projecting beyond, as stamens from the tube of the flower.

evergreen: of plants with persistent green leaves for two or more growing seasons.

F

fascicled: with a cluster of flowers, leaves etc. arising at ± the same point.

fibrous: matted with fibres or old leaf remains.

filament: the stalk of a stamen supporting the anther.

filiform: thread-like, long and slender.

foliolate: having leaflets.

follicle: fruit formed from a single carpel usually opening only along the inner suture to which seeds are attached.

G

geophyte: a plant with perennating organs (e.g. bulbs) underground.

glabrous: devoid of hairs, smooth.

glandular: with secreting structures.

globose: nearly spherical.

H

habitat: natural environment of an organism; the place where it is usually found.

head: compact mass of flowers or florets.

hemiparasite: a plant that can produce its own organic material, but receives water and salts from its host.

herb: a plant lacking a definite firm, woody structure.

herbaceous: referring to plants having the same characteristics as herbs.

hooded: helmet-like, e.g. upper lobe of an orchid flower.

I

indefinite: not a stated period.

indehiscent: not opening when ripe.

inflorescence: arrangement of flowers.

interpetiolar: of stipules placed between the petioles of opposite leaves.

involucre: a whorl of bracts surrounding an inflorescence.

irregular: asymmetrical, e.g. flowers or leaves that cannot be divided into two equal halves in any vertical plane.

K

keel: lower boat-shaped part of a leguminous flower.

L

lanceolate: lance-shaped, tapering towards both ends, 2 to 3 times as long as wide.

latex: usually a clear liquid exuding from cut surfaces of leaves and stems of certain plants.

lax: loose.

leaflet: one part of a compound leaf.

lenticel: a corky spot usually on young bark.

linear: long, narrow and of uniform width.

lip: lobe of a flower in which petals are fused.

lobed: divided into segments.
locule: chamber or compartment.

M

median: situated in the middle.
membranous: of thin, translucent texture.
midrib: central vein of a leaf.
moniliform: constricted laterally and appearing bead-like.
monoecious: with male and female flowers separate, but borne on the same individual plant.

N

nectar guides: floral orientation cues directing a pollinator to the nectar.
node: portion of a stem at which a leaf or leaves and accompanying organs arise.

O

obovate: the reverse of ovate, the terminal half broader than basal half.
ocrea (or ochrea): a membranous, stipular growth found in the Polygonaceae.
opposite: with two leaves at a node on opposite sides of a stem and in the same plane.
orbicular: flat with a ± circular outline.
ovate: broadly elliptic, the basal end broader.
ovoid: solid shape that is oval in flat outline.

P

palmate: of a leaf shaped like the palm and fingers of a hand.
panicle: a loosely branched inflorescence.
parasite: an organism dependent on other plants or animals as a food source.
partite: cleft nearly but not quite to the base.
pendulous: hanging down.
perennial: of a plant with a life-span of three or more seasons' duration.
persistent: remaining attached, not falling off.
petal: a unit of the corolla.
petiole: a leaf stalk.
pinna: a primary division or leaflet of a pinnate leaf.
pinnate: of a leaf divided into leaflets arranged on opposite sides of the midrib.
pod: a legume; an elongated fruit with one compartment, splitting open to reveal a row of seeds on one margin, as in a pea.
prickle: a sharp outgrowth from surface layer containing no conducting tissue.
procumbent: growing along the ground without rooting at nodes.
prostrate: a general term for lying flat on the ground.
pseudobulb: a false bulb, e.g. the thickened or bulbiform stems of certain orchids, which are solid and borne above ground.

pubescent: with short, soft hairs, down-like.

pungent: ending in a sharp, rigid point.

R

raceme: an inflorescence in which the youngest and last to open flowers are at the top.

rachis: axis bearing flowers or leaflets.

ray-florets: outer florets of some species of the Daisy Family, in which the corolla is conspicuously strap-shaped.

recurved: bent backwards.

reflexed: bent downwards or folded backwards.

rhizome: a creeping underground shoot, which usually extends horizontally.

rootstock: a subterranean stem.

rosette: a crowded, circular cluster of leaves or other organs.

runner: long, slim, prostrate shoot, rooting to form a new plant at its tip or elsewhere along its length.

S

sagittate: applied to base of a leaf or an anther with two acute, straight lobes directed downwards like in an arrow-head.

scandent: climbing without aid of tendrils.

scarious: thin and dry, not green.

sepal: a segment of the calyx.

serrate: toothed like a saw, with regular, pointed teeth.

sessile: sitting, without a stalk.

seta: a bristle or stiff hair.

shrub: a woody plant without a single main trunk, branching from the base.

simple: not divided or lobed.

sinus: angle formed by the basal lobes of a leaf.

solitary: borne singly; of a flower not associated with other flowers in an inflorescence.

spadix: a flower-spike with a fleshy or thickened axis.

spathe: leaf-like bract or sheath enclosing a flowerhead.

spathulate: spoon-shaped (narrow at the base).

spike: an inflorescence with the flowers sessile along a simple axis, with youngest flowers at the tip.

spine: a sharp-pointed, hardened structure modified from another organ.

spinescent: spine-tipped.

spur: a slender, usually hollow extension of some part of the flower.

stamen: a unit of the male whorl of a flower, consisting of the anther and filament.

staminode: an abortive stamen without a fertile anther.

standard: the large posterior, ± erect petal of a papilionaceous flower belonging to subfamily Papilionoideae of the family Fabaceae.

stellate: star-like.

stipule: leaf-like appendage at the base of a leaf stalk, usually in pairs.

stolon: a shoot that bends to the ground and takes root; a horizontal stem at or below surface of the ground that gives rise to a new plant at its tip.
stoloniferous: having stolons.
style: narrow, stalk-like extension of a pistil which extends from the ovary to the stigma.
subglobose: somewhat spherical.
subsessile: almost stalkless.
subterranean: in the earth, underground.
succulent: fleshy, able to store large quantities of moisture.

T

taproot: the main descending root of a plant that has a single dominant root axis.
tendril: coiled structure on stem or leaf, used for climbing.
tepals: any of the members of the perianth that is not differentiated into calyx and corolla.
terminal: at the apex of the stem and branches.
terrestrial: on or in the ground.
thyrse: a panicle with unlimited growth of main axis but with side branches in cymes.
translucent: transmitting light but not transparent.
transparent: easily seen through.
trifoliolate: with three leaflets.
tuber: swollen, underground storage stem.
tubercle: a small tuber, or rounded, protruding body.
tunic: a covering or any of the layers of a bulb.

U

umbel: an inflorescence in which the flower stalks arise from one point and spread out like spokes of an umbrella.
undulate: wavy.
unisexual: bearing only male or only female reproductive organs.
utricle: bladder-shaped structure, applied to the traps of *Utricularia*.

V

virgate: with many long, slender, ± straight, ascending stems.

W

whorl: a set of parts radiating from an axis.
wing: expanded ridge, on a stem or fruit; one of the side petals on leguminous (Pea or Bean Family) flower.

Literature references and further reading

ACOCKS, J.P.H. 1988. Veld types of South Africa, edn 3. *Memoirs of the Botanical Survey of South Africa* No. 57. Botanical Research Institute, Pretoria.

ARNOLD, T.H. & DE WET, B.C. 1993. Plants of southern Africa: names and distribution. *Memoirs of the Botanical Survey of South Africa* No. 62. National Botanical Institute, Pretoria.

COMPTON, R.H. 1976. The Flora of Swaziland. *Journal of South African Botany,* Suppl. Vol. No. 11.

DYER, R.A. 1975. *The genera of southern African flowering plants* 1. Department of Agricultural Technical Services, Pretoria.

DYER, R.A. 1976. *The genera of southern African flowering plants* 2. Department of Agricultural Technical Services, Pretoria.

FABIAN, A. & GERMISHUIZEN, G. 1982. *Transvaal wild flowers*. Macmillan South Africa, Johannesburg.

FABIAN, A. & GERMISHUIZEN, G. 1997. *Wild flowers of northern South Africa*. Fernwood Press, Vlaeberg.

HENDERSON, M.R. & ANDERSON, J.G. 1966. Common weeds in South Africa. *Memoirs of the Botanical Survey of South Africa* No. 37. Department of Agricultural Technical Services, Pretoria.

LEISTNER, O.A. 2000. Seed plants of southern Africa: families and genera. *Strelitzia* 10. National Botanical Institute, Pretoria.

MOORE, P. 1987. Wild flowers. *A Mitchell Beazley Nature Handbook*.

ONDERSTALL, J. 1996. *Sappi wild flower guide*: Mpumalanga & Northern Province. Dynamic Ad, Nelspruit.

RETIEF, E. & HERMAN, P.P.J. 1997. Plants of the northern provinces of South Africa: keys and diagnostic characters. *Strelitzia* 6. National Botanical Institute, Pretoria.

RUTHERFORD, M.C. & WESTFALL, R.H. 1994. Biomes of southern Africa: an objective categorization. *Memoirs of the Botanical Survey of South Africa* No. 63. National Botanical Institute, Pretoria.

SMITH, C.A. 1966. Common names of South African plants. *Memoirs of the Botanical Survey of South Africa* No. 35.

Department of Agricultural Technical Services, Pretoria.

VAN WYK, B. & MALAN, S. 1988. *Field guide to the wild flowers of the Witwatersrand & Pretoria region*. Struik, Cape Town.

WELLS, M.J., BALSINHAS, A.A., JOFFE, H., ENGELBRECHT, V.M., HARDING, G. & STIRTON, C.H. 1986. A catalogue of problem plants in southern Africa. *Memoirs of the Botanical Survey of South Africa* No. 53. Department of Agriculture and Water Supply, Pretoria.

Index of scientific names

Abrus precatorius subsp. *africanus* 37
Abutilon angulatum var. *angulatum* 113
Acalypha peduncularis 193
ACANTHACEAE 13, 56, 126, 150, 176, 194
Achyranthes aspera var. *aspera* 73
Achyrocline stenoptera 130
Acrotome angustifolia 46
A. hispida 46
Adenia glauca 203
Adenium multiflorum 84
Aeollanthus rehmannii 48
Aerva leucura 33
AGAPANTHACEAE 145
Agapanthus inapertus subsp. *inapertus* 145
Agelanthus natalitius subsp. *zeyheri* 32
Ageratum houstonianum 152
Agrimonia procera 101
Ajuga ophrydis 169
Albuca glauca 200
A. setosa 28
Alepidea longifolia var. *longifolia* 40
ALLIACEAE 13, 28, 155
Aloe arborescens 186
A. branddraaiensis 186
A. davyana see *Aloe greatheadii* var. *davyana*
A. greatheadii var. *davyana* 68
A. lutescens 92
A. nubigena 93
A. verecunda 186
Alysicarpus rugosus subsp. *perennirufus* 79
AMARANTHACEAE 13, 33, 73
AMARYLLIDACEAE 13, 31, 68, 93, 187
Ammocharis coranica 70
ANACARDIACEAE 13, 39
Ancylobotrys capensis 42
Androcymbium melanthioides var. *subulatum* 26
Aneilema hockii 154
Annesorrhiza flagellifolia 120
Anomatheca grandiflora see *Freesia grandiflora*
Ansellia africana 95, 96
A. gigantea see *Ansellia africana*
ANTHERICACEAE 27

Anthericum angulicaule see *Chlorophytum angulicaule*
A. fasciculatum see *Chlorophytum fasciculatum*
A. transvaalense see *Chlorophytum transvaalense*
Antherotoma phaeotricha 165
APIACEAE 13, 40, 120
APOCYNACEAE 13, 42, 84, 122, 165, 197, 204
APOCYNOIDEAE 84
Aptosimum elongatum 172
A. lineare 149
ARACEAE 14, 26, 68
Araujia sericifera 42
Argemone ochroleuca subsp. *ochroleuca* 98
Argyrolobium tomentosum 106
Aristea woodii 146
ASCLEPIADACEAE 13
Asclepiadoideae 42, 85, 122, 165, 197, 204
Asclepias adscendens 85
A. albens 205
A. aurea 122
A. brevipes 198
A. dissona 166
A. eminens 205
A. gibba var. *gibba* 205
A. monticola 198
ASPARAGACEAE 14, 30
Asparagus cooperi 30
A. laricinus 30
A. suaveolens 30
ASPHODELACEAE 14, 26, 68, 91, 92, 186
Aspidoglossum lamellatum 197
Aster bakerianus 62
A. harveyanus 181
A. lydenburgensis 62
ASTERACEAE 14, 61, 89, 128, 152, 179, 195
Athrixia phylicoides 182
Aulojusticia see *Siphonoglossa linifolia*

Babiana hypogea var. *hypogea* 156
BALSAMINACEAE 14, 82
Barleria meyeriana 176
B. obtusa 150
B. pretoriensis 177
Basananthe sandersonii 40
Becium angustifolium 51

B. filamentosum 51
B. obovatum subsp. *obovatum* var. *galpinii* 52
B. obovatum subsp. *obovatum* var. *obovatum* 171
Begonia sutherlandii 117
BEGONIACEAE 14, 117
Berkheya insignis 141
B. pinnatifida subsp. *ingrata* 142
B. radula 142
B. setifera 142
Berula erecta subsp. *erecta* 41
BIGNONIACEAE 14, 55, 125
Blepharis saxatilis 150
Blumea aurita see *Pseudoconyza viscosa*
Bonatea speciosa var. *antennifera* 202
Boophone disticha 69
BORAGINACEAE 15, 44, 147
Bothriocline laxa 179
Bowiea volubilis 200
Brachystelma circinatum 205
BRASSICACEAE 15, 75
BUDDLEJACEAE 15, 42
Bulbine abyssinica 91
B. narcissifolia 91

Caesalpinioideae 17
Callilepis laureola 65
CAMPANULACEAE 15, 61, 151, 178
Campuloclinium macrocephalum 89
CAPPARACEAE 15, 35, 75, 99
CARYOPHYLLACEAE 15, 17, 34, 74
Catophractes alexandri 55
Cephalaria zeyheriana 60
Cerastium arabidis 34
Ceratotheca triloba 176
Ceropegia crassifolia var. *crassifolia* 166
Chaetacanthus costatus 56
Chamaecrista mimosoides 101
Chascanum hederaceum var. *hederaceum* 45
C. incisum 45
C. latifolium var. *latifolium* 169
Chironia palustris subsp. *transvaalensis* 84
C. purpurascens subsp. *humilis* 84
Chlorophytum angulicaule 27
C. fasciculatum 27
C. transvaalense 28

Chrysanthemum leucanthemum see *Leucanthemum vulgare*
Chrysocoma ciliata 130
Cineraria sp. 136
C. fruticetorum ined. see *Cineraria* sp.
Cirsium vulgare 185
Clematis brachiata see *Clematis oweniae*
C. oweniae 35
Clematopsis scabiosifolia subsp. *stanleyi* 159
Cleome angustifolia subsp. *petersiana* 99
C. hirta 75
C. maculata 76
C. monophylla 35
C. rubella 76
Clerodendrum triphyllum var. *triphyllum* 148
CLUSIACEAE 15, 116
Clutia monticola var. *monticola* 38
Coccinia adoensis 127
COLCHICACEAE 15, 26, 90
Commelina africana var. *africana* 90
C. benghalensis 144
C. eckloniana 144
C. erecta 144
C. livingstonii 145
COMMELINACEAE 15, 90, 144, 154
Commicarpus pentandrus 159
COMPOSITAE 14
Conostomium natalense var. *glabrum* 178
CONVOLVULACEAE 16, 43, 85, 123, 147, 166
Convolvulus sagittatus 43
Conyza aegyptica 129
C. podocephala 129
Corchorus asplenifolius 112
Corycium nigrescens 197
Cosmos bipinnatus 66
Crabbea angustifolia 57
Crassocephalum crepidioides 183, 195
Crassula alba var. *alba* 190
C. capitella subsp. *nodulosa* 35
C. capitella subsp. *sessilicymula* 36
C. setulosa var. *setulosa* 36
C. vaginata subsp. *vaginata* 100
CRASSULACEAE 16, 35, 99, 190
Craterostigma plantagineum 149
C. wilmsii 86
Crinum bulbispermum 69

C. lugardiae 31
Crocosmia aurea var. *aurea* 94
C. paniculata 188
Crossandra greenstockii 194
Crotalaria brachycarpa 104
C. distans subsp. *distans* 104
C. laburnifolia subsp. *australis* 105
C. lanceolata 105
C. sphaerocarpa 105
CRUCIFERAE 15
CUCURBITACEAE 16, 60, 127
Cyanotis lapidosa 154
C. speciosa 145
Cycnium adonense 54
C. racemosum 87
C. tubulosum 87
Cynoglossum austroafricanum 147
Cyphia stenopetala 61
Cyrtanthus bicolor 187
C. breviflorus 93
C. contractus 187

Dalechampia capensis 111
Delosperma sutherlandii 74
D. herbeum 74
Dianthus basuticus subsp. *basuticus* var. *basuticus* 75
D. mooiensis subsp. *mooiensis* var. *mooiensis* 75
Dicerocaryum senecioides 88
Dichilus lebeckioides 104
Dicliptera clinopodia 177
Dicoma anomala 185
D. zeyheri subsp. *zeyheri* 185
Dierama galpinii 156
Dimorphotheca jucunda 184
D. spectabilis 184
Dipcadi gracillimum 200
D. marlothii 196
D. viride 201
DIPSACACEAE 16, 60
Disperis fanniniae 31
D. tysonii 71
Dissotis canescens 164
Dolichos angustifolius 192

Eclipta prostrata 65
Elephantorrhiza elephantina 101
Emilia transvaalensis 184
Endostemon tereticaulis 170
Epaltes gariepina see *Litogyne gariepina*
Epilobium hirsutum 83
Erica woodii 84
ERICACEAE 16, 84

Eriosema nutans 108
E. psoraleoides 108
E. salignum 109
E. simulans 109
ERIOSPERMACEAE 16, 93
Eriospermum flagelliforme 93
Erodium cicutarium 80
Erythrina zeyheri 192
Eucomis autumnalis subsp. *clavata* 201
Eulophia aculeata subsp. *huttonii* 71
E. angolensis 96
E. clavicornis var. *clavicornis* 158
E. foliosa 202
E. leontoglossa 96
E. ovalis subsp. *bainesii* 96
E. tuberculata 97
E. welwitschi 97
Eupatorium macrocephalum see *Campuloclinium macrocephalum*
Euphorbia striata var. *striata* 111
EUPHORBIACEAE 16, 38, 81, 111, 193
Euryops pedunculatus 140
Evolvulus alsinoides 147

FABACEAE 16, 36, 76, 101, 159, 190
Felicia clavipilosa subsp. *transvaalensis* 63
F. filifolia subsp. *filifolia* 181
F. mossamedensis 128
F. muricata subsp. *muricata* 63
Flemingia grahamiana 109
Floscopa glomerata 154
Freesia grandiflora 188

Galium capense subsp. *garipense* 127
Gazania krebsiana subsp. *serrulata* 67
Geigeria burkei subsp. *burkei* var. *burkei* 134
G. burkei subsp. *burkei* var. *hirtella* 134
GENTIANACEAE 17, 84, 121
GERANIACEAE 17, 37, 79, 161
Geranium multisectum 161
G. wakkerstroomianum 37
Gerbera ambigua 67
G. jamesonii 195
G. kraussii see *Gerbera ambigua*
G. piloselloides 143
G. viridifolia subsp. *viridifolia* 67
GESNERIACEAE 17, 88

Gladiolus crassifolius 70
G. dalenii 188
G. elliotii 157
G. longicollis subsp. *platysepalus* 95
G. papilio 157
G. permeabilis subsp. *edulis* 157
G. pretoriensis 158
G. woodii 196
Gloriosa superba 90
Gnidia caffra 117
G. capitata 118
G. kraussiana var. *kraussiana* 118
G. microcephala 118
G. sericocephala 118
G. splendens 119
Gomphocarpus fruticosus 43
Gomphostigma virgatum 42
Graderia subintegra 86
Gunnera perpensa 193
GUNNERACEAE 17, 193
GUTTIFERAE 15

Habenaria filicornis 201
Haemanthus humilis subsp. *hirsutus* 68
Haplocarpha scaposa 141
Harbenaria nyikana 202
Hebenstreitia comosa 54
Helichrysum acutatum 130
H. argyrolepis 63
H. argyrosphaerum 64
H. aureolum 130
H. aureonitens 131
H. aureum var. *monocephalum* 131
H. caespititium 64
H. callicomum 131
H. cerastioides var. *cerastioides* 64
H. coriaceum 131
H. lepidissimum 65
H. mimetes 132
H. mundtii 132
H. nudifolium 132
H. obductum 132
H. odoratissimum 133
H. oreophilum 133
H. pilosellum 133
H. platypterum 65
H. rugulosum 89
H. setosum 133
H. splendidum 134
H. wilmsii 89
Heliophila carnosa 75
Heliotropium steudneri 44

Hemizygia albiflora 49
H. canescens 50
H. foliosa 171
H. modesta 85
H. persimilis 50
H. pretoriae subsp. *pretoriae* 50
H. transvaalensis 86
Hermannia boraginiflora 83
H. coccocarpa 164
H. depressa 193
H. grandistipula 115
H. lancifolia 115
H. parvula 115
H. quartiniana subsp. *quartiniana* 83
H. transvaalensis 116
Hermbstaedtia linearis 73
Herschelianthe baurii 147
Hesperantha coccinea 188
Hibiscus aethiopicus var. *ovatus* 114
H. calyphyllus 114
H. meeusei 114
H. microcarpus 163
H. pedunculatus 82
H. trionum 39
Hirpicium bechuanense 141
HYACINTHACEAE 17, 28, 146, 155, 196, 200
Hybanthus enneaspermus 164
Hypericum aethiopicum subsp. *sonderi* 116
H. revolutum 116
Hypochoeris radicata 143
Hypoestes forskaolii 57
H. triflora 58
HYPOXIDACEAE 17, 93
Hypoxis argentea var. *argentea* 93
H. iridifolia 94
H. obtusa see *Hypoxis iridifolia*
H. rigidula var. *rigidula* 94

ILLECEBRACEAE 17, 33
Impatiens hochstetteri subsp. *hochstetteri* 82
I. sylvicola 82
Indigastrum costatum subsp. *macrum* 77
Indigofera daleoides var. *daleoides* 191
I. filipes 76
I. heterotricha 77
I. hilaris 77
I. melanadenia 191
I. oxytropis 191
I. setiflora 192
I. sordida 77

I. zeyheri 36
Inezia integrifolia 135
Ipomoea bathycolpos 166
I. crassipes 167
I. gracilisepala 85
I. hochstetteri 44
I. magnusiana 85
I. obscura var. *obscura* 124
I. ommaneyi 167
I. papilio 167
IRIDACEAE 18, 70, 94, 146, 156, 188, 196

Jamesbrittenia accrescens 199
J. aurantiaca 173
J. grandiflora 173
Jasminum breviflorum 41
J. fluminense 41
Jatropha lagarinthoides 81
Justicia anagalloides 58
J. betonica 58
J. flava 126

Kalanchoe paniculata 99
K. rotundifolia 190
K. thyrsiflora 100
Kleinia fulgens 195
K. longiflora 67
Kniphofia albescens 27
K. linearifolia 92
K. porphyrantha 92
K. rigidifolia 92
Knowltonia transvaalensis var. *transvaalensis* 34
Kohautia amatymbica 59
K. cynanchica 59
K. virgata 178
Kyphocarpa angustifolia 73

LABIATAE 18
Lablab purpureus subsp. *uncinatus* 161
Lactuca capensis see *Lactuca inermis*
L. inermis 153
LAMIACEAE 18, 46, 85, 124, 148, 169
Landolphia capensis see *Ancylobotrys capensis*
Lannea edulis var. *edulis* 39
Lantana rugosa 168
Lapeirousia sandersonii 146
Ledebouria cooperi 155
L. revoluta 155
LEGUMINOSAE 16
LENTIBULARIACEAE 18, 125

Leonotis ocymifolia var. *schinzii* 124
Lessertia stricta 78
Leucanthemum vulgare 66
Leucas glabrata var. *glabrata* 47
Lightfootia denticulata see *Wahlenbergia denticulata*
LILIACEAE 14, 15, 16, 17, 18, 28
Lilium formosanum 28
Limeum fenestratum var. *fenestratum* 33
Limosella longiflora 53
LINACEAE 18, 110
Lindernia wilmsii 150
Linum thunbergii 110
Lippia rehmannii 45
Litogyne gariepina 182
Littonia modesta 91
L. rigidifolia 91
Lobelia angolensis 61
L. flaccida subsp. *flaccida* 151
L. flaccida subsp. *mossiana* 152
LOBELIACEAE 18, 61, 151
LOGANIACEAE 15
Lopholaena coriifolia 182
LORANTHACEAE 18, 32, 189
Loranthus 32
Lotononis eriantha 102
L. listii 102
Lotus discolor subsp. *discolor* 106
Ludwigia octovalvis 119

MALPIGHIACEAE 18, 111, 162
MALVACEAE 19, 39, 82, 113, 163
Manulea crassifolia subsp. *crassifolia* 125
MELASTOMATACEAE 19, 164
Melhania prostrata 115
Melilotus alba 36
Menodora africana 121
Mentha longifolia subsp. *polyadena* 170
MENYANTHACEAE 19, 122
Merremia palmata 123
MESEMBRYANTHEMACEAE 19, 74
Mimosoideae 17
Mimulus gracilis 53
Miraglossum pilosum 198
M. pulchellum 198
MOLLUGINACEAE 19, 33, 97
Momordica balsamina 60
Monopsis decipiens 152
Monsonia angustifolia 37, 79
M. attenuata 80
M. burkeana 80

M. glauca 37
Moraea moggii subsp. *moggii* 94
M. thomsonii 156
Mystacidium capense 31

Nemesia fruticans 86
Neorautanenia ficifolius 160
Nerine platypetala 69
Nidorella anomala 128
N. auriculata 128
N. hottentotica 128
N. resedifolia subsp. *resedifolia* 129
Nolletia rarifolia 129
Notoniopsis fulgens see *Kleinia fulgens*
NYCTAGINACEAE 19, 159
Nymphaea nouchali var. *caerulea* 147
NYMPHAEACEAE 19, 147
Nymphoides thunbergiana 122

Ocimum americanum var. *americanum* 51
Oenothera glazioviana 119
O. indecora subsp. *indecora* 120
O. rosea 83
O. tetraptera 40
OLEACEAE 19, 41, 121
Oligocarpus calendulaceus 140
ONAGRACEAE 20, 40, 83, 119
Orbeopsis lutea subsp. *lutea* 123
O. melanantha 199
ORCHIDACEAE 20, 31, 70, 95, 147, 158, 197, 201
Ornithogalum saundersiae 29
O. seineri 29
O. tenuifolium subsp. *tenuifolium* 30
Osteospermum calendulaceum see *Oligocarpus calendulaceus*
O. striatum 140
Otiophora cupheoides 59
OXALIDACEAE 20, 81, 110
Oxalis corniculata 110
O. obliquifolia 81
Oxygonum dregeanum subsp. *canescens* var. *linearifolium* 32
O. sinuatum 32

Pachycarpus schinzianus 43
Pancratium tenuifolium 31
Papaver aculeatum 99
PAPAVERACEAE 20, 98
Papilionoideae
PASSIFLORACEAE 20, 40, 203
Pavonia burchellii 113

P. columella 82
P. transvaalensis 114
Pearsonia cajanifolia subsp. *cryptantha* 103
P. sessilifolia subsp. *filifolia* 103
P. sessilifolia subsp. *marginata* 103
PEDALIACEAE 20, 88, 176
Pelargonium alchemilloides 38
P. dolomiticum 38
P. luridum 81
Pentanisia angustifolia 150
P. prunelloides subsp. *prunelloides* 151
Pentarrhinum insipidum 199
Pergularia daemia var. *daemia* 166
PERIPLOCACEAE 13
Periplocoideae 165
Persicaria attenuata subsp. *africana* 72
P. lapathifolia 72
P. limbata 72
P. serrulata 72
Petalidium aromaticum var. *aromaticum* 56
Peucedanum magalismontanum 120
Phymaspermum acerosum 135
Phytolacca octandra 73
PHYTOLACCACEAE 20, 73
Piloselloides hirsuta see *Gerbera piloselloides*
PLANTAGINACEAE 20, 59
Plantago lanceolata 59
Plectranthus grandidentatus 48
P. laxiflorus 48
P. neochilus 171
P. rubropunctatus 49
P. verticillatus 49
PLUMBAGINACEAE 21, 41
Plumbago zeylanica 41
Plumerioideae 42
Pollichia campestris 33
Polygala albida 38
P. amatymbica 162
P. hottentotta 162
P. uncinata 163
P. virgata var. *decora* 163
POLYGALACEAE 21, 38, 162
POLYGONACEAE 21, 32, 72, 189
Portulaca quadrifida 189
PORTULACACEAE 21, 74, 97, 189
Portulacaria afra 74
Psammotropha myriantha 97

Pseudarthria hookeri var. *hookeri* 78
Pseudoconyza viscosa 182
Pseudognaphalium oligandrum 63
Pterodiscus speciosus 176
Pulicaria scabra 134
Pycnostachys reticulata 149

RANUNCULACEAE 21, 34, 98, 159
Ranunculus baurii 98
R. multifidus 98
Raphionacme hirsuta 165
Rhigozum brevispinosum 125
Rhynchosia adenodes 107
R. monophylla 107
R. nervosa var. *nervosa* 107
R. nitens 108
ROSACEAE 21, 101
Rubia horrida 127
RUBIACEAE 21, 59, 127, 150, 178
Ruellia sp. aff. *Ruellia patula* 57
Rumex acetosella subsp. *angiocarpus* 189

Salvia runcinata 148
S. tiliifolia 148
SANTALACEAE 21, 32
Sarcostemma viminale subsp. *viminale* 122
Satureja biflora 47
Satyrium cristatum var. *cristatum* 70
S. longicauda var. *longicauda* 71
S. neglectum subsp. *neglectum* 71
Scabiosa columbaria 60
Scadoxus puniceus 187
Schistostephium artemisiifolium 135
S. crataegifolium 136
Schizoglossum bidens subsp. *productum* 204
S. cordifolium 204
Schizostylis coccinea see *Hesperantha coccinea*
Scilla natalensis 146
S. nervosa 29
Sclerochiton harveyanus 177
SCROPHULARIACEAE 22, 53, 86, 125, 149, 172, 194, 199
Scutellaria racemosa 170
Sebaea grandis 121
S. macrophylla 121
S. sedoides var. *sedoides* 122
Selago capitellata 174
S. densiflora 54

S. muddii 55
S. procera 174
S. tenuifolia 55
Senecio apiifolius 136
S. bupleuroides 136
S. coronatus 137
S. erubescens var. *crepidifolius* 183
S. gerrardii 153
S. gregatus 137
S. inaequidens 137
S. inornatus 137
S. laevigatus var. *integrifolius* 138
S. lydenburgensis 138
S. microglossus 138
S. oxyriifolius 139
S. pentactinus 66
S. pleistocephalus 139
S. polyodon var. *subglaber* 183
S. speciosus 184
S. venosus 139
Senna italica subsp. *arachoides* 102
Sesamum alatum 88
Sida cordifolia 113
S. dregei 113
S. ternata 39
Silene burchellii var. *burchellii* 74
S. undulata 34
Siphonoglossa linifolia 178
Sisyranthus randii 199
SOLANACEAE 22, 52, 172
Solanum panduriforme 172
S. sisymbriifolium 172
S. supinum 52
S. tomentosum var. *coccineum* 52
Solenostemon latifolius 149
Sopubia cana var. *cana* 87
Sphedamnocarpus pruriens subsp. *pruriens* 111
Sphenostylis angustifolia 79
Stachys aethiopica 47
Stenoglottis fimbriata 158
STERCULIACEAE 22, 83, 115, 164, 193
Stomatanthes africanus 62
Streptocarpus dunnii 88
Striga asiatica 194
S. bilabiata 175
S. elegans 125, 194
S. forbesii 87
S. gesnerioides 176
Stylosanthes fruticosa 106
Sutera caerulea 173
S. neglecta 174

Talinum arnotii 97
T. caffrum 98
Tapinanthus rubromarginatus 189
Taraxacum breviscapum 143
Tenaris chlorantha 123
Tenrhynea phylicifolia 89
Tephrosia capensis 78
T. elongata var. *elongata* 106
T. longipes subsp. *longipes* 159
T. rhodesica 160
Tetraselago wilmsii 175
Teucrium trifidum 46
Thesium cytisoides 32
Thunbergia atriplicifolia 126
T. neglecta 56
THYMELAEACEAE 22, 117
TILIACEAE 22, 112
Trachyandra asperata var. *swaziensis* 26
T. margaretae 27
Triaspis hypericoides subsp. *nelsonii* 162
Tribulus terrestris 110
Trichodesma physaloides 44
Tricliceras longepedunculatum var. *longepedunculatum* 117
Tridax procumbens 135
Trifolium africanum var. *africanum* 190
Tritonia nelsonii 95
Triumfetta rhomboidea var. *rhomboidea* 112
T. sonderi 112
T. welwitschii var. *welwitschii* 112
Trochomeria debilis 127
Tulbaghia acutiloba 155
T. leucantha 28
TURNERACEAE 22, 117

UMBELLIFERAE 13
Urginea multisetosa 196
U. sanguinea 29
Ursinia nana subsp. *leptophylla* 140
Utricularia cf. *arenaria* 125
U. stellaris 126

Vahlia capensis subsp. *vulgaris* var. *linearis* 100
VAHLIACEAE 22, 100
Vellozia 155
VELLOZIACEAE 22, 155

Verbena bonariensis 168
V. tenuisecta 168
V. venosa 169
VERBENACEAE 22, 45, 148, 168
Vernonia colorata subsp. *colorata* 61
V. fastigiata 179
V. galpinii 179
V. myriantha 180
V. natalensis 180
V. oligocephala 180
V. poskeana subsp. *botswanica* 180
V. staehelinoides 181
V. sutherlandii 181
V. wollastonii 62
Veronica anagallis-aquatica 175
Vigna frutescens subsp. *frutescens* var. *frutescens* 160
V. vexillata var. *vexillata* 161
VIOLACEAE 23, 164
VISCACEAE 23, 203
Viscum combreticola 203
V. rotundifolium 203

Wahlenbergia denticulata 178
W. krebsii subsp. *krebsii* 179
W. undulata 151
W. virgata 61
Walafrida densiflora see *Selago densiflora*
W. tenuifolia see *Selago tenuifolia*
Waltheria indica 116
Watsonia transvaalensis 70

Xenostegia tridentata subsp. *angustifolia* 124
Xerophyta humilis 155
X. retinervis 156
XYRIDACEAE 23, 90
Xyris gerrardii 90
Xysmalobium asperum 165
X. parviflorum 197
X. undulatum 204

Zaluzianskya elongata 53
Zantedeschia albomaculata subsp. *albomaculata* 26
Z. rehmannii 68
Zinnia peruviana 195
Zornia capensis 107
ZYGOPHYLLACEAE 23, 110

Index of common names

Aambeibos 185
Aandblom 40, 59, 83
Aandblommetjie 59, 157
African Cucumber 60
African Wild Clover 190
Afrikaanse Klawer 190
Agrimony 101
Akkermonie 101
Alfileria 80
Alsbos 79
Alsbossie 80
Amarabossie 180
American Groundsel 184
Angelbossie 80
Apple of Sodom 172
Aster 135

Bakbossie 129
Balbossie 118, 121
Balsam Apple 60
Balsamina 60
Barberton Daisy 196
Barleria 150
Baswortel 101
Beesbossie 130, 182
Beesdubbeltjie 88
Bergbietou 184
Bergkruie 136
Berglelie 70
Besembos 118, 156
Besembosse 42, 139
Beukesbossie 45
Bietou 141, 184
Bird's Brandy 168
Bitter Apple 172
Bitterappel 172
Bitterbos 60
Bitterhout 204
Bitterwortel 43, 84, 204
Blaasoppies 43
Black-eyed Susan 39
Bladder Flower 42
Bladder Hibiscus 39
Bladderweed 39
Bladderwort 126
Blou-Angelier 146
Bloubittertee 180
Bloublom 176
Bloublommetjie 63
Bloudissel 98
Blou-ertjie 160
Blougifbossie 182

Bloukappie 163
Bloupoeierkwassie 145
Blouselblommetjie 144
Blouslangkop 146
Bloutee 179, 181
Blouteebossie 179, 181
Bloutou 184
Blouwaterbossie 168
Blouwaterlelie 147
Blue Bitter Tea 180
Blue Hyacinth 146
Bobbejaandruif 73
Bobbejaangif 127, 203
Bobbejaanstert 156
Bobbejaantou 43
Bobbejaanuintjie 156
Boesmanrietjie 142
Boesmanstee 182
Bokhara Clover 36
Bokhorinkie 198
Boot-Protector 88
Bosbloutee 180
Botterblom 98
Brandblare 34, 172
Brandbossie 130
Brandlelie 187
Brooms and Brushes 193
Burweed 73
Bush Tea 182
Bushman's Tea 182
Bush-violet 150
Butter Lily 91
Buttercup 98

Californian Poppy 99
Canary Weed 137
Candelabra Flower 69
Cape Ivy 138
Cape Poison Bulb 69
Cape Saffron 173
Carpet Flower 172
Cat's Whiskers 171
Caustic Bush 122
Caustic Creeper 122
Chaff Flower 73
Chinese Bur 112
Chinkerinchee 29
Chocolate Bells 44
Common Dubbeltjie 110
Common Gazania 67
Common Mealie-witchweed 194
Common Storkbill 80
Conyza 129
Cooper's Squill 155
Coral-bead Plant 37
Cosmos 66
Cotton Milkbush 43
Crab's Eyes 37
Crane's Bill 79
Creeping Lady's Sorrel 110
Creeping Sorrel 110
Crimson Flag 188
Curry Bush 116

Dense-thorned Bitter Apple 172
Devil's Thorn 88
Digdoringbitterappel 172
Disseldoring 185
Dog Daisy 66
Doll's Powder-Puff 145
Doll's Protea 185
Donkieperske 199
Doringpapawer 99
Doringtamatie 172
Dubbeltjie 88, 110
Duiweltjies 88
Dysentery Herb 37
Dysentery Weed 80

Eclipta 65
Eland's Bean 101
Elandsboontjie 101
Elandsertjie 102
Eland's Senna 102
Eland's Wattle 101
Elandswortel 101
Elephant's Root 101
Ereprys 175
Ertappeluintjie 156
Evening Primrose 40, 83, 120

Ferweelboontjie 78, 108
Fire Lily 187
Fish-bone Cassia 101
Flame Lily 90, 188
Flannel Weed 113
Forest Inkberry 73
Fynblaarverbena 168

Gansies 43

Garden Ageratum 152
Geelappel 172
Geelblombos 135
Geelboslelie 90
Geelbossie 182
Geelkeurtjie 108
Geelklawer 102
Geelklits 101
Geelklokkies 91
Geellusern 104
Geelopslag 137
Geelplakkie 100
Geelslangkop 91
Geelwateruintjie 122
Geitabossie 37
Gewone-dubbeltjie 110
Gewone-mielierooi-blom 194
Giant Mealie Witchweed 87
Gifappel 172
Gifbol 69, 70
Gifbolletjie 201
Gifbossie 118
Gombossie 83
Granny Bonnet 31
Griekwatee 67
Griekwateebossie 67
Grondboontjie 102
Grootklits 73
Groot-mielierooi-blom 194
Ground Bulb 86
Gryshout 185
Gunpowder Plant 74

Haakdoring 30
Hairy Wild Lettuce 143
Harige-skaapslaai 143
Hartblaartaaiman 113
Heartleaf Sida 113
Hibiscus 114
Highveld White Vygie 74
Hottentot's Tea 132
Hottentotskooigoed 133
Hottentotskooikruie 133
Hottentotstee 132

Impala Lily 84
Impalalelie 84
Inkberry 73
Inkbessie 73
Inkblom 54
Ink Plant 54
I Spy 171

Jakkalsbos 185
Januariebos 118

Kafblom 73
Kalwerbossie 185
Kankerblare 98
Kanniedood 189
Kapokmelkbossie 43
Karoobossie 130
Katbossie 30
Katstert 54
Katstertjie 73
Keitabossie 37
Kerrieblom 118
Kerriebos 116
Kleingousblommetjie 67
Kleingrysbitterappel 52
Kleingrysbitterappeltjie 52
Kleintongblaar 59
Kleinvarkblom 26
Klimop 35
Klitsbossie 112
Knoppiesvermeerbos 134
Kopseerblom 69
Kopseerblommetjie 194
Kortdoringgranaat 125
Kosmos 66
Krimpsiekteblaar 29
Kruitbossie 74

Langbeenbossie 179
Large Mealie-witchweed 194
Laventelbos 45
Lemoenbloeisels 35
Leopard Orchid 95
Lighted Candles 32
Lily 28
Lobster Flower 171
Lucky Bean 37

Maagbitterwortel 185
Maagbossie 112
Margriet 66
Marguerite 66
Mealie Crotalaria 105
Meidebossie 116
Melkbol 42
Melkbos 122
Melkgras 111
Melktou 122
Mexican Poppy 98
Mielie-crotalaria 105
Mieliegifbol 187
Milkweed 43, 111

Milkwood 111
Mistletoe 203
Mock Scabious 60
Moederkappie 31
Moles' Spectacles 86
Monkey's Tail 156
Montbretia 94
Mooinooientjie 76
Moon Daisy 66
Morning Bride 60
Moss Verbena 168
Moth Catcher 42
Motvanger 42
Mushroom Flower 54
Muskuskruid 80

Naaldebossie 37
Nagblom 120
Narrow-leaved Ribwort 59
Natal Primrose 126
Nenta Kalanchoe 190
Nentabos 190

Olifantstert 156
One-day Flower 167
Oondbos 129
Oorlosie 80
Opklim 199
Orange River Lily 69
Ordeal Bean 164
Otterbossie 42
Ouma-se-groottoon 200
Ox-eye Daisy 65, 66

Pale Bluebell 151
Patrysblom 26
Persvarkblom 68
Peultjiesbos 99
Pine-leaved Verbena 168
Pink Lady's-slipper 164
Plakkie 190
Plantain 59
Ploegbreker 192
Plough-breaker 192
Pluimbossie 159
Pluisbossie 182
Poison Apple 172
Poison Tree Vernonia 180
Pom-pom Weed 89
Pompombossie 89
Poprosie 64
Porkbush 74
Porselein 189
Pretty Lady 76
Purple Arum 68
Purple Top 168

Purple Witchweed 176
Pusley 189
Pyjama Flower 26

Ragwort 136
Rankbossie 43
Ranksuring 110
Rasperdissel 142
Red Arum 68
Red-hot Poker 92
Red Poppy 99
Redstar Zinnia 195
Rehmann Lippia 45
Rhodesian Foxglove 176
Rice Flower 60
River Pumpkin 193
Rivierlelie 69
Rivierpampoen 193
Rooiblom 87, 194
Rooiblommetjie 176
Rooiboslelie 90
Rooigousblom 195
Rooi-opslag 193
Rooskleurige-nagblom 83
Rosary Pea 37
Rose Evening Primrose 83
Royal Paintbrush 187
Ruikbossie 173

Sabie Star 84
Saffraanbossie 173
Sambokbossie 67
Scotch Thistle 185
Seeroogbossie 116
Sewejaartjie 64
Sheep Sorrel 189
Short-thorn Pomegranate 125
Silky Burweed 73
Silver Bullet 104
Single-leaved Cleome 35
Skaamblommetjie 201
Skotse Dissel 185
Skullcap 170
Slangappel 52
Slangappeltjie 52
Slangkop 29, 44, 91
Smalweëblaar 59
Sore-eye Flower 69
South Coast Bushviolet 150
Spantou 122
Spear Thistle 185
Speelwonderboom 64
Spekboom 74
Spider Flower 35

Spider-leg 113
Spindlepod 35
Spinnekopbossie 112
Spotted Knotweed 72
Spurge 111
Star Bladderwort 126
Steenboksuring 110, 189
Sterblasiekruid 126
Stinkkruid 129
St John's Wort 116
Superb Lily 90
Sutherland's Curse 113
Swartdoring 55
Sweet Clover 36
Sybossie 137

Taaibloublommetjie 63
Tandpynbossie 41
Teebossie 79, 131
Terblansbossie 39
Thorny Poppy 99
Tiger Orchid 95
Tjienkerientjee 29
Tobacco Witchweed 176
Tontelbossie 141
Toothache Root 41
Toy Sugarbush 185
Traveller's Joy 35
Tree Orchid 95
Tridax Daisy 135
Tuin-ageratum 152
Tuinranksuring 110
Tulp 93
Tumbleweed 70

Uurblom 39

Vaalbossie 131
Veerbossie 159
Veld Onion 28
Veldpatat 159
Velskoenblaar 68
Vermeersiektebossie 134
Vervain 169
Viltige-duisend-knoop 72
Vingerhoedblom 176
Vingerhoedbossie 176
Violet-of-the-Karoo 172
Voëlbrandewyn 168
Voëlent 203

Waaierbossie 112
Waterereprys 175
Waterlily 147
Water Parsnip 41
Water Speedwell 175

White Evening Primrose 40
White-flowered Mexican Poppy 98
White Lady 100
Wild Acalypha 193
Wild Apricot 42
Wild Asparagus 30
Wild Aster 63, 181
Wild Begonia 117
Wild Bindweed 43
Wild Buttercup 98
Wild Clover 190
Wild-cowpea 161
Wild Dog 159
Wildeappelkoos 42
Wilde-ertjie 161
Wildejakobregop 195
Wildeklawer 190
Wildeknoflok 26
Wildekomkommer 199
Wildemargriet 65
Wildepapawer 99
Wildepatat 124
Wildepatatta 167
Wildeperske 42
Wildepieterselie 120
Wildestokroos 114
Wildeverbena 168
Wild Everlasting 64
Wildewinde 167
Wild Foxglove 88, 176
Wild Lasiandra 164
Wild Lucerne 106
Wild Parsley 120
Wild Peach 42
Wild Penstemon 86
Wild Petunia 124
Wild Purslane 189
Wild Scabious 60
Wild Spinach 127
Wild Squill 146
Wild Sweetpea 161
Wild Tomato 172
Wild Verbena 168
Wild Violet 172
Witbergvygie 74
Witblom-bloudissel 98
Witchweed 87, 194
Witgousblommetjie 67
Witnagblom 40
Witstinkklawer 36
Wolbossie 64
Woolflower 73
Wurmbossie 129

Yellow Lily 91
Yellow-seed 108
Yellow Sorrel 110
Yellow Wandering Jew 90